D1095655

THE RELAXED SELL

The

ILLUSTRATIONS BY ROBERT OSBORN

THOMAS WHITESIDE

Relaxed Sell

NEW YORK · OXFORD UNIVERSITY PRESS · 1954

Of the articles in this book the following appeared originally in *The New Yorker:* 'The Relaxed Sell,' 'The Amphibious Pen,' and 'No Lobster Men from Neptune,' copyright 1950, 1951, 1952 by Thomas Whiteside.

'Wired for Sentiment' appeared in *The Reporter*, copyright 1953 by Thomas Whiteside; 'Life Can Be Terrible,' 'The Smoke-filled Barn,' and 'Commercial Composers' in the *New Republic*, copyright 1947, 1948 by Thomas Whiteside.

The author wishes to express his thanks to *The New Yorker, The Reporter*, and *New Republic* for the kind co-operation extended to him.

PRINTED IN THE UNITED STATES OF AMERICA

To Marie

CONTENTS

The
Relaxed
SELL

AS a television viewer, I have sometimes found myself taking a greater interest in the compelling oratory and accompanying panorama of flying beer bottles, zooming candy bars, exploding containers of breakfast foods, singing cough drops, and animated coffee cups that make up the commercials than in the programs themselves. Consequently I decided, one day, to investigate this restless new art form and the creative processes of the advertising people who are developing it. My first move was to get in touch with Jack Denove, an account executive of Batten, Barton, Durstine & Osborn, the advertising agency for the American Tobacco Company, makers of Lucky Strikes. The Lucky Strike commercials, it seemed to me, were fairly representative. I had watched cigarettes as they marched, did square dances, climbed in and out of packages, and lit themselves — action every second. Mr. Denove, I had been informed, was in charge of advertising for Lucky Strikes. I called him up, explained to him what I wanted, and he invited me to come over to his office the following morning.

Denove's office was a large room with rich green walls, carpet an inch deep, green upholstered armchairs, a green leather sofa, and an enormous desk cluttered with proofs of Lucky Strike ads. Behind the desk was a phonograph turntable built into a tier of shelves. When I arrived, the room was full of people. Denove, a short, bouncy man with curly hair, shot out of the chair at the great desk and shook hands. 'Nice to have you drop in,' he said. 'We've just been having a little get-together with the television boys here. I'd like you to meet them.' He then introduced several men, all of whom were with B.B.D.O.: Jim Campbell and Warren Schloat, writers of television commercials; Hugh Rogers, chief of television production; Dan Lownsberry, a producer of television commercials; and Bob Olds, who I gathered was an 'expediter' of television commercials. After the introductions, they retired to a corner to examine a film on a Movieola, a machine for editing

4

films, and Denove and I sat down. 'Television is the most amazing, the most terrific thing in America,' Denove said. 'We're working against the clock. B.B.D.O. has forty clients in television. We've been turning out commercials at the rate of one a day. We have B. F. Goodrich, we have Schaefer Beer, we have Fort Pitt Beer, we have My-T-Fine desserts. And, of course, we have Lucky Strike cigarettes. Every cigarette company has jumped into television with both feet. Chesterfield has "Arthur Godfrey and His Friends" and the Chesterfield Supper Club, with Perry Como. Camel has the Camel News Caravan, the Ed Wynn Show, and "Man Against Crime." Old Golds are in big with the "Original Amateur Hour" and half of "Stop the Music." Pall Mall's in there with "The Big Story," and Philip Morris is in with "Candid Camera." We've jumped in with "Your Lucky Strike Theatre," a one-hour dramatic show that runs every other week, on Monday nights at nine-thirty, over NBC. The show was sold to us by Robert Montgomery, who produces it and occasionally stars in it. It has an audience rating of thirty-five. That means that thirty-five out of every hundred people viewing television when the show is on are tuned in to "Your Lucky Strike Theatre." We have six minutes of commerical time on the show. Maybe you wouldn't think it, but we have to put in more effort — more stage work, more acting, more people, more time, and more rehearsal — per minute on those six minutes than we do on anything else we do on the air. It's terrific.'

Denove's expression suddenly turned from one of enthusiasm to one of pain. He was looking at the lighted cigarette that I held in my hand. 'I see you're smoking a Chesterfield,' he said. 'We like people to smoke Luckies around B.B.D.O.' I hastily put out my cigarette, and he offered me one of his.

'We've just started a new campaign for Luckies,' he went on. He leaned back in his chair, raised his eyes to the ceiling, and recited the slogan of the new campaign: 'Let your own taste and throat be the judge. For smoothness and mildness, there's never a rough puff in a Lucky Strike.' Then he sat up and said, 'We have the rough-puff story on radio seven days a week. And, of course, on TV. Camels are running the Thirty-Day Test on TV. They use society sportswomen and superimpose the T-Zone over their throats as they deliver their endorsements. But nobody has told the fine-tobacco story like Luckies. We spell that out in "L.S. —— M.F.T. —— Lucky Strike Means Fine Tobacco." Fine tobacco means consumer satisfaction. We spell out consumer satisfaction in smoothness and mildness. Pardon me.' Two men had just entered the office and were striding up to Denove's desk — George Moses, the B.B.D.O. copy chief for the Lucky Strike account, and Harry Olsen, the agency's art director for the account. They had a stack of Kodachrome transparencies with them, and they began to show them to Denove.

'If it's not sexy, it's no good,' said Denove jovially.

'How's this?' asked Olsen, holding a transparency up to the light.

Denove was dubious. 'Here,' he said to me, handing over the picture. 'Is that sexy enough?'

It showed Hedy Lamarr dressed in peacock feathers. I said she seemed very attractive.

'O.K.,' Denove said. 'We'll use it in the magazines. That's a dress she wore in *Samson and Delilah*.'

'Sure, let the Bible tell 'em,' said someone or other.

'Get it downtown today,' Denove said.

I remarked to Denove that all the cigarette advertisements I could remember seeing showed people not smoking but

6

merely holding lighted cigarettes, but that this form didn't seem to apply to cigarette commercials on television. 'No, it doesn't at all,' he said. 'They actually *smoke* them in television. You don't show people smoking in still ads because the cigarette would hide the face. See what I mean?' Denove held one hand up to his mouth. 'It doesn't look good. But smoking looks wonderful in television. Smoking is an *instantaneous* act.' Denove lit a Lucky, leaned back, and gracefully demonstrated the principle. 'Look. You put your cigarette up to your face. You take your puff in the normal manner — watch me — and you blow out the smoke. It takes a couple of seconds. Then you see the person's face again. What could be more natural?'

The group of men clustered in the corner began to drift out of the office. 'Say, Hugh!' Denove called out to Rogers, the production chief, a young man with a splendid head of hair and a diagonally striped collegiate tie. 'I had a sudden ulcer at nine-twenty-eight last night. People could have tuned out "Lights Out" and switched stations to "The Goldbergs" without knowing there was a Montgomery show on the air. Typical problem,' he said sidewise to me. 'We start the show with the words "Robert Montgomery Presents" on a title card. His name is too long! It won't fit into one line that will show up on that small screen. People can hardly read the lettering.'

'We're reviewing the title-card situation now,' said Rogers. Denove then suggested that I talk with Rogers about the problems involved in producing television commercials, and that I sit in with Campbell and Schloat, the writers, while they wrestled with ideas for commercials for the next Montgomery show. I said I'd enjoy doing that.

After lunch, I went to Rogers' office. On one of its walls was pinned a large floor plan of a television studio. A two-foot-high cardboard cutout of a pack of Lucky Strikes, the sides of which slanted down in false perspective, stood on the floor against another wall. 'I used to be with CBS,' Rogers said when I asked him about himself. 'I was a T.D. — technical director. I helped build up "Mr. I. Magination" as competition to "Kukla, Fran, and Ollie," on NBC. High-class kid show. I helped build up "Lucky Pup" from a ten to a twenty-nine audience rating. Got out of the network deal just at the right time. When television was getting under way after the war, the networks figured that they, and not the advertising agencies, were going to control sponsored programs. Well, I don't know. I gave it a lot of thought and decided to go over to the agency end. What a business! Everything you do in television is new. No matter what you try, it's never been done before.'

I asked him how things were going on the Lucky Strike program.

'The rough puff is a damn difficult thing to make anything visual out of,' he said. 'By the way, we had quite a session over whether to spell it "r-u-f-f." It seemed more symmetrical. I was all for it, but Jack Denove overruled me. As a matter of fact, a small, simple, inanimate object like a cigarette can't just be exhibited. With commercials for some consumer goods, like refrigerators, you just change the words and the actors every week and keep your set the same, and the refrigerator can just sit there, while its features are pointed out. You don't *have* to move it around. With cigarettes, you can't point out features, you have to show more than the cigarette itself; we have to change the basic set every time. Everything we do runs into a terrifying amount of dough. In fact, everything anybody does in television runs into a terrifying amount of dough. In radio, you could put a show on with five people, outside of the actors. Now, consider the Lucky Strike show on television. I figured

8

out that in the Montgomery show there are two hundred and fourteen separate jobs to be done. These are carried out through the combined facilities of NBC, the Montgomery organization, and B.B.D.O.'

Rogers ticked off the jobs on his fingers. 'First,' he said, 'you have thirty-nine property men and technicians on the studio floor. You have five men in the film studio, which is over in Radio City, to run off films. You have seven cameramen and five cameras — two of them push camera dollies. You have eight electricians and electrical-prop men, two dressers, a makeup man, and a scene painter — and he just touches up what someone else has already done. In the control room, you have an audio man, a technical director, an assistant technical director, a turntable man, a sound-effects man, the show director, the commercial director, and a few fellows from B.B.D.O. And then you have whole departments behind these people — film-slide men, artists, shoppers for props, trucking concerns, scene designers, carpenters, and painters. And you have at least a dozen other B.B.D.O. men working back at the agency. You probably have a hundred and fifty people directly involved in just this one show. Plus, of course, the actors for the play and for the commercials.'

Rogers pointed to the floor plan. 'That's where we do the Lucky Strike show,' he said. 'The studio is on West Sixty-seventh Street. Used to be a stable. The ground floor is leased for two days a week by NBC, which leases it from ABC.'

Only half of B.B.D.O.'s commercials, Rogers told me, are presented 'live.' The other half are put on film. While costs vary a good deal, a one-minute live commercial costs B.B.D.O. an average of about seven hundred and fifty dollars to produce, not including talent, whereas a one-minute commercial on film

9

costs a thousand dollars. 'A film spot is more expensive, but it's safer,' he said. 'If an actor makes a fluff, you can reshoot the scene. If he makes a boner on a live commercial, there's nothing you can do about it. Not long ago, Dennis James, the announcer, was over at Madison Square Garden covering the Dog Show for Du Mont. James had to deliver a pitch for dog food, so we got the cameras on this dog and James offered it a bowl of the dog food. The dog had taken it nicely during rehearsals, but when it came to the actual commercial, he refused to even look at the stuff. James practically had to ram it down the dog's throat.' He went on to tell me about Morey Amsterdam, a comedian, who, while smoking a cigarette on the Chesterfield Supper Club show to demonstrate its mild qualities, had a violent fit of coughing. 'Frankly, B.B.D.O. is pretty careful about that sort of thing,' Rogers said. 'A while back, we had a rush film commercial for Luckies. We had it made by a commercial-film outfit in Detroit, and flown here. The spot featured a boy and a girl in the shadows. They take out a couple of Luckies, light them, and you see their faces by the light. They're about to kiss when they look around, see the camera, look embarrassed, and pull down a shade in front of them. The shade has the Lucky bull's-eye on it. We looked at that film for an hour. There was something wrong; we didn't know what. Jack Denove and I decided to get out to Detroit right away. We set out for LaGuardia in a car, ran out of gas on the Queensboro Bridge, got to the airport without tickets, grabbed somebody else's seats, flew to Detroit, and went straight to the set. I talked to the girl model. I offered her a Lucky. "Sorry," she says, "I don't smoke." I realized right off what had gone wrong. The girl wasn't inhaling.'

I complimented Rogers on his quick action. 'We like

everybody to both inhale *and* exhale on our commercials,' he said. 'Stanton and Morgan, our two announcers on the Montgomery show, are inveterate smokers. They can exhale and talk at the same time. It's good, because in a one-minute commercial, a puff takes a relatively long time, and by exhaling and talking at the same time, Stanton and Morgan can keep the action going at the clip we want.'

The telephone rang. Rogers picked up the phone and talked into it for a few moments. 'Those smoke rings don't look so hot,' he finally remarked into the mouthpiece. 'Can't we do something about it?' After he had hung up, I expressed interest in the smoke-ring problem. 'We made a sixty-second film spot of a girl smoking a Lucky,' Rogers explained. 'She was supposed to blow smoke rings into the camera lens. She couldn't blow them the way we wanted her to, so we had phony rings dubbed into the film by optical printing. Smoke rings are a terrible problem. We turned up this guy in Detroit — Peterson, I think his name was — who claimed to be able to blow twenty-six smoke rings at a time. We had our production people check on him for a live commercial. It seemed like a swell idea, and everything was going nicely when we realized that the studio air-conditioning and all the hot lights would set up air currents that would disintegrate the smoke rings as soon as they were out of Peterson's mouth. I talked to the Peterson guy over long distance. He said that if we would build him a glass cage to blow his smoke rings in, no air currents would bother him. That sounded reasonable enough until we realized that we couldn't photograph through glass, on account of the reflections.'

Rogers walked over to the Lucky Strike cutout. 'This is one of our standard props,' he said. 'Notice the dull finish. A shiny surface causes terrific halation on the television screen. So does white. Notice that the pack has been painted in shades of gray. Can't use the Lucky Strike red. Some image-Orthicon pickup tubes in the television cameras are red-sensitive — everything goes to white. And white causes halation, too. We just had to knock out a white cow from the prop list of an upcoming show for that reason.'

I asked about the false perspective of the cutout.

'That's a carry-over from our still ads,' Rogers said. 'When you see a picture of a Lucky pack in a magazine, it's drawn in false perspective so that you can see the "L.S./M.F.T." on the bottom. The client spends millions of dollars on little touches like that in the magazines, so we have our display packs on television commercials made with the same false perspective. Have you ever noticed the way the cigarettes come out in a Lucky ad?' Almost every cigarette advertisement, of no matter what brand, shows a pack with a few cigarettes sticking out. Chesterfield sometimes has all the silver foil torn off and three cigarettes pulled out. Camel shows the foil unfolded, not torn, and a row of cigarettes in a pyramid arrangement. Lucky Strike has four cigarettes popping up asymmetrically. 'Anyway, we like to see the big packs in our commercials in false perspective,' Rogers said. He looked at his watch.

I said I was thinking of going over to talk to the television writers.

'We don't *have* any television writers yet,' he said. 'They're really radio writers trying to get the hang of a new medium. As soon as we get a writer in for television copy, the first thing he does is grab a dictionary of television terms, and then he throws everything at you. Triple superimpositions, involving three or four camera takes on half a dozen words —

12

gee, the T.D. couldn't call the shots that fast — fancy dissolves, windshield wipes, pop-through wipes, iris wipes, barn-door wipes, double-barn-door wipes. That's for film. You can't do most of the wipes on live television. You know what wipes are — where one scene is taken off the screen by a moving line, revealing another scene. In a film, one wipe can cost you two hundred bucks. But you get a budget of a thousand dollars for a one-minute film commercial and the writers throw in a wipe every two seconds. It kills you! They ask you for crowds. In television, five people are a crowd! I've seen ten people in a television shot and I swear to God that on the screen they looked like a hundred milling around. Once, some writers wanted a giant pack of Luckies that everybody would climb out of through the Lucky bull's-eye. They called for one fourteen feet high. It sounded fine, but if something like this were viewed on the average set, the action would be so far away from the camera that you wouldn't be able to recognize the people climbing out of the pack. Anyway, you have to keep all the action in the center of the screen, away from the critical zone at the edges, where the image gets fuzzy. Usually, you have to count on losing 8 per cent of the vertical image and 13 per cent of the horizontal.'

After thanking Rogers for talking to me, I went to see Campbell and Schloat, the television, or radio, writers. They were huddled together at a desk in a tiny room. On one wall was a chart of what looked like Navy signal flags.

'That's a chart of wipes,' said Campbell, a scholarly looking man of about thirty. 'This is a barn-door wipe, this is an iris in, this is an iris out.'

'We use wipes a good deal for film spots,' said Schloat, a round-faced man of about the same age.

'I have a dictionary of television terms, if you'd like to go through it sometime,' Campbell said. I thanked him and asked how he and Schloat were coming along with the next Lucky Strike television commercial.

Schloat said they had submitted several tentative scripts. 'The first opens with Bob Stanton — he's one of our announcers — building his own props in the studio,' Campbell said. 'He's sawing away at something in a vise and chanting, in rhythm with the sawing, "Never a rough puff, never a rough puff, never a rough puff." That got thrown out downtown by Mr. Vincent Riggio himself. Mr. Riggio is chairman of the board of the American Tobacco Company. Then we tossed them a new script, with the rough-puff line, to go with an animated film of a bunch of cigarettes doing a barn dance. Jack Denove has the thing downtown right now for approval.'

'We did one that showed Ray Morgan — he's our other announcer — and Stanton at a cigarette counter,' said Schloat. 'They see a buyer undecided about which brand he's going to buy. They put on an act about smoothness and mildness, and the guy finally buys a pack of Lucky Strikes. And that got thrown out.' He turned to Campbell. 'We've got to get some ideas.' Both men sat and thought for a few minutes. I didn't interrupt.

'I have one,' Schloat finally said. 'We'll get Morgan in a room — he's at home — with a picture behind him. The picture comes to life and delivers the commercial. We could do it through rear projection onto a movie screen.'

'The production boys are going to kill us,' said Campbell. 'Maybe the picture could be a tobacco-growing scene. The picture starts to animate and you have a bunch of these independent tobacco experts delivering their opinions about Lucky

Strike. Morgan says, "Boy, they know what they're talking about!" and goes into the rough-puff pitch. Wait — I'm thinking of a topper. The picture dissolves to a shot of a girl. I don't know — do we have a beautiful girl on film saying something good about Lucky Strike?'

'Maybe we could work in one of the early planters,' Schloat suggested.

'Let's not go into tobacco history,' Campbell said.

Bob Olds, the television-commercial 'expediter,' came into the office.

'Do we have a girl on film talking about Luckies?' asked Campbell.

'No,' said Olds.

'When I worked for Walt Disney, I used to spend three months on a six-minute scene,' said Schloat. 'This pace staggers me.'

'Do you see any possibilities in a thirty-thousand-buck coronet they crowned Dorothy Kirsten with at the Richmond Tobacco Bowl Festival?' asked Olds. 'Sinatra in person, and stuff.'

'No,' said Campbell.

Olds walked out, and another man rushed in. 'Just got back from downtown,' he said. 'They won't take the barn dance.'

'My God!' Campbell cried.

'Geez!' said Schloat.

'What did he say?' Campbell asked.

'He said he didn't like it,' replied the man from downtown. 'He just said, "Let your own taste and throat be the judge. For smoothness and mildness, there's never a rough puff in a Lucky Strike." Said that four times.'

'V.R. said that?' Campbell asked in a whisper.

'Four times,' said the man from downtown, and vanished.

Campbell and Schloat looked harried. 'We have a minute-long film around somewhere,' said Campbell. 'It isn't the cutest in the world, but it shows a lot of people smoking.'

'We'll probably have to work nights this week,' Schloat remarked.

'I'm on every girl I know's black list,' Campbell said.

'Maybe Jack will think of something,' Schloat said.

'Morgan is in the studio, and his fairy godmother goes "Ping!" and delivers his commercial for him,' Campbell suggested, a little desperately.

The telephone rang. Campbell picked it up. 'Jack's back. Let's go see him,' he said, and I trailed after them.

As Campbell, Schloat, and I walked into Denove's office, he was putting down on the floor beside his desk a huge zippered briefcase of the type called, in the advertising profession, a presentation case. A presentation case generally contains charts and is considered indispensable by topflight advertising men. 'I would like you to hear something terrific,' Denove said as we all sat down. He unzipped his case, took out a large acetate record, and put in on the turntable behind his desk. A blast of sound came out that shook me. A troupe was singing, in operatic style, a song about Lucky Strike's fine tobacco. 'Wonderful, isn't it?' cried Denove, bouncing in his chair. 'It hasn't been approved yet, but I think it'll go great on radio, and maybe we could do something with it on television.'

Rogers walked in. Denove turned off the phonograph.

'We're thinking of a rear-projection scheme — ' Schloat began.

'Morgan's at home,' Campbell broke in. 'He has this picture framed. The picture animates. Maybe we could have Joe Burnett — he's sold fine tobacco for Luckies. He says, "I've sold millions of pounds of tobacco, but none so smooth and mild as Lucky Strike." '

'No,' said Rogers firmly. 'None of that. We can't get the equipment.'

Schloat and Campbell looked disappointed. For a few minutes, everyone thought intently. 'An idea,' Rogers said, finally. He paced up and down through the deep carpet. 'We open with a closeup of workmen's feet dangling in mid-air — ' he said.

'He wants feet,' Denove murmured to the room at large.

'From the feet,' Rogers went on, 'we pull the camera up to two workmen sitting on a girder five hundred feet in the air above New York. They take out their lunch, then light up with Luckies. Then right along the girder walks Morgan and delivers the commercial. It would make a sweet spot.'

Denove shook his head slowly.

Undaunted, Rogers tried again. 'Have Morgan and his wife rehearsing his commercial,' he said. 'She says, "I think you ought to say, 'There's *never* a rough puff in a Lucky.' " He says, "No, dear, it's 'There's never a *rough* puff.' " And so it goes.'

'Good!' cried Denove. 'Let's try that out. And for the second commercial let's get F. E. Boone, our independent tobacco auctioneer. Let him explain what his Lucky Strike chant is all about. And get a girl with him. I'll call F.E. down South and fix it up.'

The meeting then broke up, with many expressions of optimism.

On the way out of Denove's office, Rogers said it might

17

be interesting for me to talk to Robert Foreman, vice-president in charge of radio and television copy. I said I would like to, and Rogers led me to another office and turned me over to Foreman, a short, dapper man wearing a crisp bow tie, who had been banging away at an ancient typewriter. 'Sit down,' said Foreman. 'I've just been working on a company speech. Last year, the B.B.D.O. slogan was "You've got to be good to be big." This year, it's "To stay ahead takes thinking ahead." Now, if you don't mind listening a while, I have some people to see.' Foreman glanced past me toward the door, and two young men in shirtsleeves, their hands full of papers, came forward. 'These are what we call story boards,' Foreman said to me. 'When we begin a television commercial, and particularly a film commercial, we rough out the action in a series of pictures on the left side of the page, and the audio text on the right. If the story board is approved, we send it to several commercial-film producers — there are hundreds of them waiting to grab business in television — for estimates.'

One of the young men put his load of story boards on Foreman's desk. 'This first set happens to be a series of television commercials we're preparing for Schaefer Beer to use on the Dodger games this season,' Foreman told me. 'We've done some good work for Schaefer in the past. We had the camera drink a glass of Schaefer. The beer pours right over the screen. For Meister Bräu, we had the camera drink a glass of beer *and* eat a hamburger. The hamburger rises, fills the screen, and comes down with a great bite out of it. On a Wildroot Cream-Oil spot, we had a girl kiss the lens. And for the American Tobacco Company, we had the lens smoke a Lucky. A very effective gimmick.'

Foreman turned to the two young men. 'You want to show

18

the Cleveland Indians through a glass of beer after the second inning?' he said. 'O.K. But can we use the names of the players during a commercial? Are we invading their right of privacy?' He picked up his phone. 'That was one of our legal eagles,' he said to me when he had finished. 'You see the kind of thing we're up against. That gag about the wife who sees her husband over television at a baseball game with a blonde — it's a real problem for us. Where do we stand when we superimpose a beer bottle on a crowd scene? Can a guy in the crowd sue us? We have to be careful. I guess I'll decide about these Schaefer spots later.'

The two young men left, and two others came in and sat down. They, too, were in shirtsleeves.

'Let's have it,' Foreman said.

The two men cleared their throats and, tapping out time, loudly sang a jingle in praise of Calso, a gasoline.

'It'll do,' said Foreman. The two young men departed. 'Sung to the tune of "Little Brown Jug," ' Foreman told me with satisfaction. 'A public-domain tune. It saves us dough. We have them orchestrated on the outside. But on television we're only allowed to use orchestration — orchestration in the usual sense, that is — in our live commercials.'

I asked Foreman what he meant. He explained that in 1944 James C. Petrillo forbade all members of the American Federation of Musicians to record music on film for television. Most of the jingles for television were therefore being sung *a cappella* or to an accompaniment of instruments beneath the notice of Petrillo. 'The ukulele, for instance, isn't recognized by Petrillo as a musical instrument,' said Foreman. 'We use ukes a good deal, as well as the tipple, which is a uke strung with steel strings and sounds somewhere between the guitar and the balalaika.

We can use jew's-harps, kazoos, the goofus, kids' glass xylophones, toy pianos, and sand blocks, which are just a couple of pieces of sandpaper-covered wood you rub together for rhythm. As a matter of fact, I think Petrillo's cracked down on sand blocks lately. He claims they're a musical instrument. We also use human voices to imitate some instruments banned by Petrillo. Some of our people can dub in a bass fiddle by blowing a "puck-puck-puck" sound close to the mike. There's one guy who does the snare drum, trumpet, and sax by breathing through his nose. He must be making a small fortune out of TV sound tracks.'

Most of the lyrics B.B.D.O. uses in television commercials are written there in the office. 'We do everything from Gilbert-and-Sullivan-type things to Rodgers-and-Hammerstein-type things,' Foreman said. 'We do a swell Bromo-Seltzer train that puffs smoke. The smoke puffs have numbers — one, two, three. Fights headaches and stomach distress three ways — get it? We videoize the radio thing wherever we can. Of course, testimonials are something of a problem. On the radio, you can just quote them. On the Jack Benny program, for example, the announcer comes on, gives a pitch for Luckies, then says, "As Ray Bolger recently remarked . . ." And another voice quotes Bolger on how he likes Luckies. You can't impersonate anyone on television. You have to get your people in person, and too many of them have contract clauses preventing them from appearing. We're working on that problem. We've had a plan to use Dorothy Kirsten on a Lucky Strike film spot. The commercial would open with the usual words, "Let your own taste and throat be the judge"; then we'd switch to a shot of a judge on the bench, banging his gavel. I forget the rest of it.' Foreman got up from his chair and pointed to a chart on the wall. 'Do you know what these are?' he asked.

'Wipes,' I said. I thanked him and headed for the elevator.

One morning, I went up to the Sixty-seventh Street studios; 'Your Lucky Strike Theatre' was going on the air that night. The studio it was to be broadcast from was a huge room crisscrossed halfway down from the ceiling with a complex of steel scaffolding from which hung scores of klieg lights on lattices. Carpenters were hammering. Television cameras on dollies were being pushed around. A group of people were standing in the middle of the stage chatting. Rogers wasn't there, but I picked out Dan Lownsberry, the producer of television commercials — and went up to him. 'The actors for the commercials will be here in a few minutes,' he said. 'There have been some changes. The commercial with the emphasis in the rough-puff line was thrown out downtown at the last minute. We substituted another, and *that* was thrown out. The final one we worked out involves a cartoon film of marching tobacco leaves. We'll show Morgan and his wife watching the film on their television receiver, and Morgan delivering his pitch in the form of remarks about the leaves. That's the set, there.' Lownsberry pointed to a corner of the studio. The set consisted of a backdrop, painted to represent a living room, and two armchairs, a coffee table, and a low bookcase, which was evidently to serve as the television receiver. In the middle of the studio was a tremendous backdrop of blue paper. 'F. E. Boone's setup for the second commercial,' Lownsberry said. 'We'll have him do his chant in the middle of some big Lucky packs hung from the scaffolding. A sort of abstract idea. Something like a Dali painting.'

A well-built man of about sixty, with white hair gray at the sides, came in. He turned out to be F. E. Boone himself. 'Mighty glad to meet you,' he said to me. He looked around. 'My, my, what an interesting place. I've never done a television show before. They tell me the show starts at nine-thirty. I'm going to miss my ten-thirty train back to Richmond.' 'F.E. doesn't really need a script,' Lownsberry whispered as Boone slid out of his topcoat. 'He has this thing taped backward, forward, and sideways. On radio, we use him to warm up the audience before the "Hit Parade" show. Ask him for a sixty-second spiel and he'll give you a minute on the button.'

The studio began to fill up. One of the arrivals was Bob Stanton, a stocky man with a mustache. He was carrying a briefcase, which he threw on the floor. The other announcer, Ray Morgan, a tall, slender fellow, came in immediately afterward, and *he* threw a briefcase on the floor. Stanton cleared his throat and did an imitation of a tobacco auctioneer's chant. 'Gee, I did a swell commercial for the Mohawk Carpet show on tele last week,' he told Lownsberry. 'I had a girl sitting on my lap. She was dressed in harem-type pants. She stroked my hair while I delivered my pitch.'

Two pretty girls walked onto the floor and said hello to Lownsberry. They were Mary K. Wells and Patsy Jenkins. 'Mary plays Morgan's wife,' Lownsberry told me. 'Patsy works with F. E. Boone.'

Rogers rushed in, his arms full of big cardboard imitations of packs of Luckies. 'Get these strung up at different angles!' he yelled to the carpenters.

I approached F. E. Boone, who was standing in a corner, looking through his script. 'My goodness,' he muttered, 'what's all this? "Pack zooms to full screen, ECU Boone." I never had anything like that on radio.'

Lownsberry, who had joined us, said, 'It means "extreme closeup." '

'Thank you, sir,' said Boone.

A lawyer for the American Tobacco Company came in, and glumly took a position near the set.

'All right, we'll take a run through the Boone commercial first!' cried Rogers. 'Places!'

Miss Jenkins, Boone, and Stanton went over and stood before the blue-paper backdrop. Rogers squinted at them through a small range finder he was holding in one hand.

'L.S. —— M.F.T.!' cried Stanton, with the urgency of a police radio call. 'L.S. —— M.F.T.!'

F. E. Boone delivered the familiar Lucky Strike auctioneering chant.

'Gee, Mr. Boone, I think it sounds *terrific!*' Miss Jenkins said. 'But —— uh, what does it mean?'

'Just a minute, F.E.,' said the American Tobacco Company lawyer. 'Something just occurred to me. If you chanted that fast, would there be any implication that you were selling faster than the legal rate of four hundred baskets an hour?'

'Well, I chant at the rate of between six and seven hundred words a minute,' Boone said.

'I don't want trouble with the F.T.C.,' the lawyer said. 'The idea is you don't sell the tobacco farmers' crops like *that.*' He snapped his fingers.

'I don't try to nudge,' Boone said defensively. 'I just try to stay out of trouble.'

'All right, let it pass,' the lawyer said.

The rehearsal continued. Boone explained the meaning of

23

his chant, reciting it slowly, then speeded it up again to an unintelligible babble. At its slow pace, the chant resolved itself into something like 'At sixty, one dollar bid, and a one, and a one, and a one; at sixty-two, two dollars bid, and a two, and a two, and a two,' and so forth. I timed his explanation at one minute flat.

I walked over to Ray Morgan, who was lounging in one of the armchairs on his set.

'Smoking through all these hours of rehearsal is apt to dry you up,' Morgan said, eying the furious puffing that was going on then over on the Boone set. 'In the rehearsal for the first Montgomery show, I fogged. I had five pages of hard sell to do solo, and I had three drags to take. I wasn't easy about it. But I finally solved the problem. The trick is either to blow all the smoke out before you speak or get most of it out. I took it up with the production boys. "Let's show relaxation," I said. "Let's wait a few seconds after I take a drag. Let me blow the smoke out." The boys liked the idea. I blew the smoke out slowly, and it worked beautifully. It was a *relaxed* sell.'

Morgan lit a Lucky, blew out a cloud of smoke, and observed that he would rather work TV than radio any day. 'That camera is more like a face in front of you,' he explained. 'I'm on "The Talent Search," over NBC. Also the "Magic Clown" show, over WNBT, on Sunday mornings, right after the Horn & Hardart show. "Magic Clown" is sponsored by Bonomo's Turkish Taffy — I eat the stuff in the commercial. Regular cornball of a show. Working with kids is a cinch — you wiggle your eyes and hoke it up. I wear a fez and give out membership cards for the Bonomo Magic Club, certifying members as Junior Master Magicians. Next week, I'll be wearing guns. Never have to worry about blowing your lines on a kid show. I've got the thing woodshedded anyway. I can do the pitch backwards. As a matter of fact, this Bonomo Turkish Taffy is a damn good-tasting candy bar. It lasts forever. You'd wonder how the Bonomo people ever get any turnover with a product like that. But tele — boy, what a selling medium! Since the show started, they've had to put on two extra shifts at the Bonomo factory, and they're still six or seven weeks behind on their orders.'

I wandered off to look around the studio, which, I found, was divided into two sections, one housing sets for the two commercials and the other several sets for the play that would be done that night on 'Your Lucky Strike Theatre.' As I finished my tour, I saw that Robert Montgomery had arrived and seated himself behind a highly authoritative-looking desk on the side where the commercial sets were. I was introduced to him, and he invited me to sit down by his desk for a talk.

'Are you an expert yet?' Montgomery asked me. 'This is what I call the era of the expert in television. After a couple of weeks in the business, you're an expert.' He laughed. 'It reminds me of the days in Hollywood when sound was new. Everybody fell in love with sound. We used to have beady-eyed experts who went around knocking on the walls of fifty-thousand-dollar sets and saying, "You can't shoot sound with that in here." Everything overwritten for sound. My God, you'd have a courtroom scene with a guy in the witness box — the lawyer would ask his name and he'd make a five-minute speech. You could just see the producer telling the writer, "Gee, we've got to have him *say* something." The same thing in TV, except he says, "For God's sake, we've got to have him *do* something." '

Rogers came up to us. 'We have a terrific idea for a new commercial,' he told Montgomery, 'and we want to do it live, in the studio here soon. It would be the biggest commercial ever done. An operatic deal, where we sing out the rough-puff thing with a thirty-six-piece orchestra, a ballet troupe, and Dorothy Kirsten. Mr. Riggio loves it.'

Montgomery looked shaken. 'What —— here?' he asked in a choked voice.

'Sure,' Rogers said calmly.

Montgomery passed a hand over his forehead. 'How will the dramatic show look after an opening like that, huh? Like something out of Cedar Rapids. Oh, well, I guess we can always underplay it, with competition like that.'

'It was Jack Denove's idea,' said Rogers, as though that settled everything, and then walked away.

A prop man came by, pushing a television camera on which was painted, in big letters, 'L.S./M.F.T.' Montgomery eyed it coolly. 'You know,' he said, 'I was at a party the other night where people were split right down the line on whether they should buy television sets. Those who were against it gave all the stock arguments about not wanting their kids to be watching it all the time, but I really think they were fighting themselves. They're afraid of the temptation of this thing. And it *is* a tremendous temptation, isn't it?' He popped a stick of gum into his mouth, and began chewing.

A production assistant laid a carton of Lucky Strikes on Montgomery's desk and carefully arranged a few more packs in a sort of display. After he moved away, F. E. Boone came up and reached for a pack in the display. 'Sorry, Mr. Boone,' Montgomery said, 'those are for my opening announcement.'

'Ah'm all out,' Boone said. 'Need some more to rehearse with.'

'I bring in twelve cartons of Luckies for the show and eight are missing already,' a production man was shouting, a few feet away. 'Those damned stagehands!'

A cameraman trained his lens on Montgomery. I hurriedly got up. 'Take a look,' said Montgomery, pointing to his desk. I looked, and, on a small television screen built into the top of his desk at a slight angle, I saw my image. 'If I care to, I can watch myself on the monitor as I deliver the opening of the show,' Montgomery said. 'As it happens, I don't care to.'

Morgan was rehearsing on his set, puffing away at a Lucky in a relaxed manner. 'Let your own taste and throat be the judge,' he was telling Mary K. Wells, contentedly blowing smoke in her face.

Rogers, who was watching this rehearsal, told me that he had a new idea for a commercial. 'Stanton comes out and starts the rough-puff pitch,' he said, 'then asks, "Where's Morgan?" Meanwhile, Stanton is reaching into his breast pocket for a Lucky. Right away we dissolve to a cloth setup that looks like a king-size pocket. Morgan pokes his head out and delivers *his* commercial. He finishes by pushing an eight-foot pack out of the pocket.'

Rogers stopped to listen to Morgan's commercial. 'When you get to the sell, start pumping!' he shouted to Morgan a moment later.

I moved on to the other set, where Bob Olds and F. E. Boone were examining what appeared to be a tobacco leaf.

'What do you think, F.E.?' asked Olds.

'My goodness, it looks mighty fine,' said Boone. 'Could do with a little curl around the edges, though.'

'We make this leaf out of latex,' Olds said to me. 'Up to the last show, we were using real tobacco leaves. The company sent them up from Richmond in a steam box. The stuff had to get here moist; otherwise the leaves were liable to crumble to pieces right in the middle of the commercial. The last batch they sent up got all dried out. I tried to connect the steam box to the pipes in the basement, but I couldn't. I hung them up behind the shower curtains in the bathroom and turned on the hot water in the tub, but they still seemed so dry I didn't dare risk putting them on the show. About four hours before air time, I began to get really desperate, so I took the tobacco leaves down to the Luxor Baths in a cab. I arrived with the leaves sticking out of a bundle of newspapers and told the manager I wanted to take a Turkish bath. I took off my clothes, wrapped a sheet around me, and headed into the Turkish room. The attendant, a great big guy, wanted to know what I had with me. "Tobacco leaves," I told him. The guy just looked offended.'

I turned to F. E. Boone and remarked that he must find it difficult to get away from his tobacco auctions. 'Haven't sold tobacco for ten years,' he said. 'I'm on the "Hit Parade" now,

28

and starting soon I'll be with Frank Sinatra again. It takes me five and a half seconds to deliver my chant. I fly out to Hollywood or wherever the show is, deliver my five and a half seconds, then fly back to my farm in Kentucky. When I feel myself getting rusty, I practice my chant in the bathtub in the morning.'

I asked Boone how long he had been smoking Lucky Strikes. 'Luckies have been mah choice for eighteen years,' he answered gravely, and he moved off, under the klieg lights, toward the cameras.

LIFE
Can
Be Terrible

To unclog the national pore, American soap mills are turning out ten billion bars of soap each year. This statistic constitutes a high tribute to both the cleanliness of the population and the enterprise of our captains of industry. It is also a glowing testimonial to the genius of Frank and Anne S. Hummert of Greenwich, Connecticut, two lesser-known manufacturers without whose inspirations the American public might well slip back to apathy and distrust of soap and all that soap implies. The Hummerts, too, operate a mill, a soap-opera mill. Their

NOTE: This sketch was written at a time when the television industry had not yet begun its attempts to convey the art of the soap-opera into the confines of the home-size television screen. Since that time, versions of a few soap-operas have been presented serially on television, but the visual action has not added much to the aural dramatics well known to experienced daytime radio listeners. Time may change all this. Yet soap-operas were designed to be heard; they are of the pattern of communication that once led Mr. Alistair Cooke to characterize American radio as 'audible wallpaper.' Let us therefore dispense with the latest innovations, and go back to the immediate postwar years, when soap-opera was in its fullest flower. — T.W.

33

empire is daytime radio. With the co-operation of such patrons as the makers of Sweetheart Soap, Blu-White Soap Flakes, Bab-O, and Oxydol, the Hummerts have colonized one-eighth of all radio network time available during daylight hours to propagate sanitary habits and moral values among the house-wives of America.

In the medium of the soap-opera, more formally known as the daytime radio serial, the Hummerts have discovered and developed an art form admirably adapted to the pace and re-quirements of a machine age. They have constructed a belt-line technique of production so efficient that in one year alone their organization was able to pour out 3,640 scripts totaling six million words to put on the air their fourteen continuing soap-operas. Of the forty-two million daytime listeners in the nation, 80 per cent of them women, few can spin their dials without encountering Hummert operas like 'Ma Perkins,' 'Backstage Wife,' 'David Harum,' 'Front Page Farrell,' 'Just Plain Bill,' 'Lora Lawton,' 'Lorenzo Jones,' 'Our Gal Sunday,' 'Rose of My Dreams,' 'Stella Dallas,' 'The Romance of Helen Trent,' 'The Strange Romance of Evelyn Winters,' 'Young Widder Brown,' or 'Katie's Daughter.'

These fifteen-minute, five-times-a-week dramas are con-ceived in outline by the Hummerts, principally Anne, and writ-ten by fourteen captive playwrights. 'The operation works just like General Motors,' a network executive remarked. A Hummert aide prefers the historical approach. He has com-pared the Hummerts to Alexandre Dumas, who employed sixty apprentices to help write his 277 volumes of novels and plays. 'Not that I'd carry the analogy too far,' the Hummert man said modestly, gazing out of the window of his office.

Indeed, the Hummerts are modest to the point of silence

on the nature and scope of their operation. While willing to praise the virtues of, say, Heet liniment daily over 'The Romance of Helen Trent,' they prefer to have as little publicity for themselves as possible. It is understood that certain enemies of soap-opera have in the past placed upon the Hummert head a crown of thorns. Consequently, the Hummerts have developed a remarkably tight security system. Top echelons of the Hummert hierarchy become noticeably nervous when approached for information. Like many of the characters in their plots, they suddenly develop amnesia. Even former Hummert writers (known within the corps as 'dialoguers'), who have been expelled for deviationist activities such as amputating the leg from a character for whom the Hummerts have a certain fondness, speak only in guarded tones of their periods of enlistment.

Exploration, therefore, tends to begin with the soap-operas themselves. To thwart undue excursions into this world, the Columbia Broadcasting System, one of the great carriers of soap-operas into the home, has conveniently prepared a scientific document for the use of outside inquirers. The gist of this is that soap-operas are commendable productions, and that listeners like them anyway. In its treatise, CBS has evolved a Happiness Index into which housewives with the soap-opera habit are neatly graded. According to CBS, 85 per cent of the women approached testified that they were happy, except for a few bad moments. 'This ought to encourage us all,' the CBS document concludes.

One CBS official says she had considerable difficulty in persuading audiences to confess their addiction to soap-operas. 'They obviously listened, but wouldn't admit it,' she said. 'The exception was Memphis. All the women were quite frank about it there. The reason isn't hard to find — very little social mobility in Memphis.' Questioned individually, most soap-opera listeners who admitted their addiction explained that 'they're so true to life,' and furthermore that the dramas helped them forget that they were doing the dishes.

Thus, in holding the mirror up to nature, soap-operas abound in such natural phenomena as acid throwing, throat operations (Will Nora be able to talk again?), eye operations (Will Nora regain her sight?), and brain tumors (Will Nora recover at all?). Brain tumors as a dramatic subject seem to have been something of a Hummert specialty, and other soap-opera companies have taken them up, too. At one point, the brain-tumor epidemic even spread to Hollywood. Bette Davis developed one in the motion picture *Dark Victory*. Shortly after the movie was released, a number of women, some of them with black hats pulled to one side of the face, in the Bette Davis manner, turned up at various hospital clinics with the unshakeable conviction that they, too, had brain tumors. The symptoms they displayed came to be jocosely known to some medical men as the 'Dark Victory' syndrome. Some of the catastrophes in Hummert soap-operas are of a seasonal nature. In summer, for example, the physical-injury rate goes up considerably when the writers, to provide what is termed a 'hypo' during the slack listening season, usually arrange to have several of their characters involved in dreadful accidents. Generally, the accidents do not cause irreparable damage to the characters involved, except to minor characters considered expendable. On occasions past, however, the slaughter has been known to get out of control. The indignation of the Hummerts was considerable when, returning from Europe at the end of one summer, they discovered that one of their writers, in the absence

36

of his chiefs, had carelessly amputated the leg of Pa Wiggs, a favorite character in 'Mrs. Wiggs of the Cabbage Patch.' The latest fashion among Hummert writers is to throw assorted characters under automobiles around the end of June or the beginning of July. The characters so maltreated lie in agony until the fall season, when their wounds generally heal without their having been subjected to too drastic surgery.

The Hummert medical corps keeps well in the foreground of scientific progress. The clinical hierarchy once ordered that a character develop 'hysterical blindness' by way of a hypo. The onset of the symptoms was dramatic. Such an impression did it have on listening housewives that the character's audience rating shot up like a fever chart. 'Young Widder Brown,' another Hummert character, decided on an interesting variation of this particular maneuver. In accordance with Hummert directives she temporarily went blind because of an unfortunate allergy to chocolate cake. Her predicament was heart-wrenching to the housewives. In such situations the Hummert audience works itself up into a grievous state of anxiety, which may account for the murmurs that the Moscow Radio sometimes claims to hear from America — 'sighs and groans . . . the sorrowful cry of millions.'

Tangible evidence of audience response to soap-operas can be found in the amount of mail received by their producers. In their many years of soap-opera the Hummerts have received more than fifty million fan letters. Over an extended period of time spent listening to soap-operas, many people come to assume that some of their favorite soap-opera characters really exist. The producers of 'Front Page Farrell,' a Hummert opera involving a clever newspaper chap named Farrell, who solves all sorts of problems, once received a telegram from a woman

in the West stating her conviction that there was oil in her back yard, and that a smart man like Farrell could certainly find it if he cared to help her. She offered, of course, to pay his expenses for the trip out West.

News that a Hummert wife is about to give birth is sure to engender an avalanche of bassinets and diapers. A particular target for confidential letters is 'Ma Perkins,' a small-town busybody described in a Hummert directive as 'a woman with a heart of gold and a world of common sense . . . a philosophy of the Golden Rule . . . unselfish in her interest in individuals . . . doing unto others rather than doing others' (a personal code, incidentally, not far from that promulgated by the Borden Company for Elsie the Cow). Some time back, 'Ma' had a third child, this waif being left on her doorstep. Ma being undecided about the advisability of keeping the baby, a minister of the Gospel promptly wrote in and offered to adopt it.

So convinced are many Hummert listeners of Ma's physical existence that CBS declines even to hint that the part of

Ma is played by a professional actress. To CBS, the mere idea of revealing the actress's name approaches the bounds of sacrilege. Even the information that Ma lives in New York City rather than Rushville Center seems to them perilous. When I paid a visit to the studio for information on Ma I found CBS publicity men in a highly nervous state, and it took a certain amount of time before I could persuade them to allow me to look in on a rehearsal of 'Ma Perkins' in Studio Twenty-eight. When we arrived there, the rehearsal was just about over. A few actors were standing lethargically about the studio, and the Hammond organist was leaning his head against the console of his instrument, his eyes closed apparently in sleep.

Ma, a pleasant, gray-haired woman in her forties, was sighing into the microphone: 'But it just don't seem reasonable. What are we *ever* going to do?' 'Cut that last line,' the voice of the director ordered from the control room. 'Okey-doke,' Ma said briskly. The dialogue continued for another thirty seconds or so. Then Ma emerged from the studio, and a dynamic redhead, who had been sitting in a corner reading a newspaper, sprang to the microphone crying, 'Woo! . . . Woo! . . . That Oxydol sparkle!' In the safety of the Clients' Booth, Ma revealed that she had just finished reading her 3,621st script and was breaking into her fourteenth year as the Sage of Rushville Center, this being an occasion for presents of pillows and crocheted doilies from listeners far and wide. Some send her detailed maps of Rushville Center, and, if she is away from the show for any reason, listeners never fail to keep her informed of what has happened. During one of her recent absences a faithful listener hurriedly wrote to warn her that the local banker was up to no good.

Vacations for soap-opera actors are a bit of a problem. The Hummerts once handled this annoying interruption agreeably by arranging to have Ma held by confidence men for ransom for two weeks. In this connection, radio executives speak of one Hummert show in which the heroine was captured by savages and held in a cave gagged and bound, for her vacation period. The lady was kept in the script by having her grunt at intervals for two weeks, these moans of pain being charitably rendered into the microphone by another actress in her free moments. The audience was enthralled. Hummert writers tell of one old lady, confined to a hospital in a dying condition, who expelled her relatives from her room and rallied her last strength to listen to the climax of an episode from 'Stella Dallas.' Shortly thereafter she sank into a coma. She passed away unsatisfied, for in Hummert soap-operas only crisis follows crisis, and the last chapter is never written.

Their insight into the hopes and aspirations of American womanhood has buoyed the Hummerts through fifteen years of soap-opera. Their estimated minimum income of $300,000 a year alone testifies to a personal triumph of extrasensory perception. The Hummerts have little physical contact with the masses among whom some daily manifest, according to tests made by Dr. Louis Berg, a New York psychiatrist, such emotional reactions as tachycardia, arrhythmia, profuse perspiration, tremors, gastro-intestinal disturbances, and vertigo while listening to their productions. The Hummerts live in a large French Colonial house in Greenwich, Connecticut, and do so little entertaining that the natives regard them almost as hermits.

Frank Hummert, a tall, thin, introspective man, was born in New Orleans probably in the 'eighties. Reports of his early life are vague. He is said to have ridden for two years with the Texas Rangers. In his twenties he went to work for the St. Louis *Post-Dispatch*, dashed off feature articles, rewrote plays, and for a time ran a school for writers. World War I gave Hummert his first real chance at molding the public will. He became a copywriter, and his wartime slogan, 'Bonds or Bondage,' was enormously successful. Hummert swiftly sailed into the advertising business at the close of the war — first with the company of Lord and Thomas; then, after a time, with the Chicago firm of Blackett and Sample, to which was added the name of Hummert in 1928. There Hummert conceived the idea of the soap-opera, the first of which was 'Just Plain Bill,' the story of a village barber who still trims beards and confidence men over the airwaves. The idea gripped the imagination of public and soap manufacturer alike, and Hummert throbbed with activity and new serials. Advertising men refer to him as 'one of the early ulcer boys.'

In his early days Hummert would never allow women to work in his office. The exception to this rule was the making of the greatest team in soap-opera. Anne Ashenhurst, a good-looking young woman with high-school experience in writing a lovelorn column for the Baltimore *Sun* and Paris *Herald*, applied for and was granted a job as Hummert's secretary. Together they turned soap-opera into big business. By 1935, when Hummert married Anne after the death of his first wife, they were both vice-presidents of the company with a joint salary of about $150,000 a year.

In 1943, eight years and 30,000 episodes later, the Hummerts withdrew, soap-operas and all, from Blackett, Sample, and Hummert for reasons unclear even to the trade press, and made their way to Greenwich to direct in much the same way as previously their own factory, Hummert Radio Features.

The actual processing of Hummert soap-operas goes on within the Park Avenue offices of Air Features, Inc., an 'associated' organization peopled with half a dozen script editors who are allowed electric buzzers and secretaries. Communications between the Park Avenue boiler room and Supreme Headquarters in Greenwich are usually in writing. Anne Hummert is undoubtedly the strategist. She manages Air Features, which she visits several times weekly, Frank now being content to handle the 'American Album of Familiar Music,' 'American Melody Hour,' 'Manhattan Merry-Go-Round,' and 'Waltz Time,' musical shows of which an Irish tenor's sympathetic rendition of 'The Rose of Tralee' is typical. Hummert takes this type of art very seriously. One of his executives once informed him in high excitement that Vivian della Chiesa, a singer featured on his 'Album of Familiar Music,' had been given the chance to sing under Toscanini's direction in Brahms's *Requiem*. This, the executive suggested, would be a golden opportunity for a high-toned plug in the 'Album' program benefiting Hummert and Miss della Chiesa alike. Hummert was shocked. 'Tell me,' he asked coolly, 'does Mr. Toscanini give *me* credit on *his* programs?'

To obtain a true understanding of the nature of soap, it is necessary to understand the basic formula involved in its manufacture: the addition of fat to caustic soda to form soap and glycerine. The Hummert formula for soap-opera consists of an equally agreeable combination, wherein misery and the Golden Rule are intertwined to oil the lady listener into the satisfying confirmation of her own virtue and the hardness of her lot.

The majority of Hummert listeners being mothers, no mother on a Hummert show can be bad — and certainly not domineering. 'If a woman is evil, she must be wholly evil,' a dialoguer remarked. Mere implication of imperfect motherhood ruined one Hummert show, 'Betty and Bob.' This was the story of a jealous couple whose daily bickerings had aroused considerable interest among the listening population until the Hummerts ordered the moody pair to have a baby. The couple continued to quarrel. The result was disastrous. Listeners snapped off their radios. 'Betty and Bob,' baby and all, were given their walking papers and driven from the studio.

Few men listen to Hummert soap-operas, most of them being at work during performances. This, perhaps, is just as well. It has been calculated that in soap-opera men cause twice as much trouble as women. In any case, the agonies of Hummert heroines are seldom of their own making, but are rather the result of circumstances beyond their control, such as swindlers, pettifogging lawyers, and acts of God. Thus, as Professor Rudolph Arnheim remarked in *Radio Research*, 1942–43, a soap-opera plot evokes within the listener 'the satisfaction of being good oneself, while others unfortunately are bad. Instead of opening the road to humble self-knowledge,' he added, 'it nourishes the cheap pleasure of self-complacency.' Curiously enough, one of the editors of the book in which this unkind cut appeared, Dr. Frank Stanton, is now president of the Columbia Broadcasting System. His network carries five Hummert soap-operas, and for its time and trouble receives from advertisers a little over three million dollars a year.

In devoting themselves to the public interest, the Hummerts are glad to supply the nation with many variants of particularly dramatic stories. Indeed, the majority of Hummert soap-operas could quite simply be reduced to two, 'Stella Dallas' and 'Our Gal Sunday.'

The 'Stella Dallas' operation involves the poor mother whose heart is broken as her daughter moves on in society. Thus Stella herself is 'the true-to-life story of *mother love* and *sacrifice* in which Stella Dallas saw her beloved daughter, Laurel, marry into wealth and society, and realizing the difference in their taste and worlds went out of Laurel's life!' And 'Katie's Daughter' is 'The story of Nana Harris, the lovely young actress who lives on Park Avenue. *And* whose mother is Katie Harris — Hamburger Katie — who runs a restaurant on the waterfront! This is the story of *two worlds* — which asks the question: *How far* should a *mother sacrifice* to give her daughter advantages in life she herself never had?' According to the story directive for 'Katie,' this is 'the great American saga.'

For the other Hummert theme, 'Our Gal Sunday' sets the pace with 'the story of an orphan girl named Sunday . . . from the little mining town of Silver Creek, Colorado. Who in young womanhood married England's richest, most hand-

44

some lord . . . Lord Henry Brinthrope. The story that asks the question: *Can* this girl from a little mining town in the West find happiness as the wife of a wealthy and *titled* Englishman?' And 'Backstage Wife' spells 'The story of Mary Noble, a little Iowa girl who married one of America's most handsome *actors*, Larry Noble, matinee idol of a million *other* women — the story of *what it means* to be the wife of a famous star.'

If the strife through which Hummert ladies are compelled to go on the road to happiness is severe, so, too, is that of the writers who create them. The Hummerts demand of their dialoguers a life of fairly rigorous discipline. Hummert writers must live — for radio men — modestly. The average salary runs to about half the usual pay for daytime radio authors. Hummert men are paid by the script, thus eliminating the necessity of paying them, for example, on Christmas Day, which usually passes quietly without soap-opera. Top-echelon Hummert executives have been known to receive a box of cookies apiece for Christmas. All of them bow low to Anne Hummert's generalship and skill. An audience with Anne in her colonial office, whose blue walls exactly match the color of her eyes, is a matter of grave concern. The faces of Hummert executives have been observed to turn to a color approaching Blu-White merely upon their being informed of an impending telephone call from Mount Olympus. On such an occasion, a secretary calls up with the following curt signal: 'Please keep your line clear. Mrs. Hummert will talk to you in ten minutes.' As the critical moment approaches, the executive is likely to expel visitors, such as dialoguers with whom he has been quietly planning, say, a brain tumor, in order to brace his nerves for a few minutes before the conference begins.

For radio executives, Hummert men live withdrawn lives.

Seldom are they to be found at Toots Shor's, '21,' Colbee's, Lindy's, and other network haunts. 'They just don't eat radio,' one writer has said.

Most Hummert writers have never met their leader except upon beginning their commission. 'I shall only call you once,' Anne is likely to tell them with a genial smile, 'and that will be to tell you that I no longer need your services.' The new millhands, many of them hired through their writings in the women's pulp magazines, retire to their homes and begin their dialogues. Their main problem is to keep the 'story line,' a brief Hummert outline of the plot, alive. When the plot wears thin, they throw in a 'hypo' to expand it again. 'It's a matter of parallel lines meeting,' one writer remarked. 'It's just like the Steinmetz theory.' Sometimes Anne herself will suggest a hypo. 'I am seriously considering sending David on an overseas assignment,' she may say in a mimeographed memorandum on 'Front Page Farrell.'

Stephen, the hero of 'Life Can Be Beautiful,' has had so many hypos as to be shot full of holes. They have included (1) a trip to Europe to return a cache of stolen jewels and collect a reward; (2) meeting, according to a Hummert producer, 'a sexy dame' who (3) drugged him, causing him to develop (4) amnesia, (5) imprisoned him, and (6) tortured him, and (7) caused him to believe that his wife was dead. Not unexpectedly, Stephen is hopelessly crippled and confined to a wheelchair, the arms of which he grips and scratches with such desperate frustration that Hummert producers arranged to have this melancholy rasping sound introduced into the script at frequent intervals. Over a period of weeks, the scratching uses up a considerable amount of time — a great convenience to the soap-opera writer. Experienced Hummert writers can spin out an episode to interesting lengths. 'You kill the whole week as best you can,' said one. 'You save your best punches for Friday.' Particularly skilled writers can kill not only a week, but several. One character was kept in a revolving door for seventeen days. Bill of 'Just Plain Bill' is said to have kept a character in his barber chair for eighteen days. Another character, a lady, was left in a bathroom for four weeks. Every time she tried to emerge from this damp environment, the scene shot elsewhere.

Some Hummert writers become derailed by personal feelings. One man, after brooding for months, introduced into his scripts a mill owner with certain attributes he now considers not uncommon to the Hummert operation. In the course of time, he found to his dismay that the mill owner, a minor character in his story, became so vividly alive as to overshadow completely the central roles. The writer was informed that he had 'lost the touch' and was invited to leave the organization.

The Hummert organization has little concern for slow, tortured dialoguers. On the other hand, experienced librettists can choose their own hours for creation. There is no need to report in. Scripts can be mailed from home. Sometimes a Hummert author will sit down with a Dictaphone, dictate 50 scripts in 3 days, then rush down to Florida to quiet his nerves. This speed is made possible partly by the fact that though each Hummert soap-opera encompasses 15 minutes of air time, the actual length of dialogue, including scratching- and moaning-time, fills only 9.5 minutes or so. The remainder of the time is taken up by such important matters as 'lead-ins,' 'cow-catchers,' 'premiums,' 'hitchhikers,' 'teasers,' and, of course, Hammond organ music.

First comes the cow-catcher ('Today, when you're miserable and distressed from heartburn or that uncomfortable, overstuffed feeling of acid indigestion . . .'), then the premium ('Send today *without fail* and get, almost as a gift, the beautiful Forget-Me-Not pin David had Susan select especially for you . . .'), 'mood-music,' and the lead-in ('David has made the startling discovery that Dempsey Hale, an attractive and clever promoter, is a swindler . . .'). Then comes the dialogue, during the course of which Susan is described as lovingly fingering her Forget-Me-Not pin.

After more mood-music there follows the teaser ('Will Linda's money be recovered?'), another gentle reminder of the Forget-Me-Not pin ('Just buy a can of Bab-O. Cut the word Bab-O from the label. Mail it . . .'), and the hitchhiker: 'For free-flowing drainpipes, wash pipes every week with Lycons — L-Y-C-O-N-S.'

Under such circumstances of crowd and urgency, the Hummert writer is delighted to get public credit for his work once or twice a week. The flyleaf of the scrip on 'Stella Dallas' may read 'dialogue by Helen Walpole,' but the announcer doesn't always read it. 'These episodes,' he usually remarks at the lead-in, 'are written by Anne Hummert.' When this happens the writers don't worry unduly. After all, as the Hummert story directive for 'Ma Perkins' so wisely remarks: 'It is not money and high position that count, but what you do for others — what's in your heart.'

Commercial

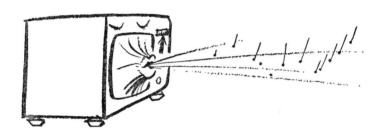

Composers

The art of the singing commercial, which advertisers so often employ to extol their products over radio and television, is an interesting one. The essentials of it are brevity of expression, singleness of theme, and an inherent ability to goad the listener into buying a particular brand of goods. Listening to singing commercials may not be easy sometimes, but neither is the task of composing them. It is a field of work that seems to require a rather special kind of skill and that is often well paid for by our industrialists. Some composers will have great artistic success with longer works and yet, turning their hand to singing commercials to make money, will fail miserably to satisfy the advertisers who commission them. The successful composer of singing commercials appears to be one with a talent ideally suited to the creation of a work lasting no longer than thirty seconds. Among the more luminous characters I have encountered during my various excursions into the shining world of radio and television are two gentlemen, Allan Bradley Kent and Austen Herbert Croom-Johnson, who not only have been professionally successful writers of singing commercials but are probably responsible, more than any of their colleagues, for bringing the art of the jingle or the spot, as singing commercials are also called in and out of the trade, to its present level of perfection. Few composers have enriched the world of commercial song so perseveringly in recent years as have Kent and Johnson. So compelling are their creations that radio programs of classical music have frequently been cut short in order that listeners might enjoy the fruits of their collaboration.

Together, during several periods of partnership extending intermittently over a number of years, Kent and Johnson have had a powerful effect on the national nerve with such brief but electrifying works as 'Momma, Momma, Won't You Larvex Me?'; 'Pepsi-Cola Hits the Spot'; and 'Listen to the Handy Flit Gun (Whistle) Sh-h-h-h-h-hhH!' Such works have been a source of considerable personal, as well as financial, satisfaction to both men. Looking back through the years with a certain tranquillity, Kent and Johnson can see themselves as the perpetuators of an honorable tradition of patronage. What Mozart was to the philanthropist Baron Von Swieten, Kent and Johnson have considered themselves to be, off and on, to such sponsors as the makers of Beechnut Chewing Gum, Esso Gasoline, My-T-Fine Desserts, Pfeiffer Beer, and Waterman's Ink. There is one significant point at which the analogy breaks down, however: Kent and Johnson have never been willing to accept the meager emoluments of composers in centuries past. Neither Kent nor Johnson has been loquacious about their income during their periods of collaboration, but Johnson once estimated that various companies had invested a minimum of two hundred million dollars in the propagation, over radio or television, of Kent-and-Johnson singing commercials such as 'Opportunity Knocks (clack, clack) on the Chipso Box' or 'To Keep Romance Alive — A Woodbury Soap Cocktail at Five' — the latter being sung to the accompaniment of ten male and female voices humming up and down. It is perhaps a tribute to the power of the singing commercial that this sum exceeds by fifteen million dollars the total monies allotted in the 1953–4 U.S. Budget for federal aid in operating public schools.

I haven't seen Kent and Johnson together for some time, but occasionally, in the past, I would drop in to see them at their business headquarters, a splendidly furnished apartment on Fifty-third Street in Manhattan. Both were usually attired in loud tweed sports jackets and gray pants, but their outward resemblance pretty well ended there. Johnson, whose precise speech, faintly baggy eyes, and noble bearing proclaimed him at once to be an English gentleman, was somewhat tall and slim, with red hair neatly brushed back. Kent was bald, except for a rim of hair extending around the sides and back of his head, and was inclined to stoutness. He wore dignified beard and might have passed, in other surroundings and dress, for a member of the French Academy were it not for his speech, which had strong overtones of Broadway.

The partners always spoke respectfully of their art. They never pronounced the opprobrious word 'jingle'; the phrase they used was 'musical announcement.' Both had a good deal to say on behalf of musical announcements, and Johnson, without much prodding, would sometimes launch into a lengthy historical discourse on that interesting subject, beginning, say, with street cries like 'Who'll Buy My Sweet Lavender' and ending perhaps with the Kent-Johnson number,

I ate too much
I ate too fast
Oh boy did I feel dismal!
It's the easy thing
For the queasy thing
Soothing Pepto-Bismol . . .

'We try to concentrate on good taste,' Johnson would tell me. Because of their joint sensibilities, the partners usually declined to accept commissions for odes to such products as deodorants or laxatives, but once, yielding to the importunities of an advertising agency, they consented to dedicate themselves in a small way to personal daintiness, and turned out a musical commercial beginning 'Underarm can be charming' and sentimentally rendered by several girls in close harmony.

'Mr. Kent says "With this one we just knock on the door, we don't break it down," ' the composers' secretary told me one afternoon after playing a record of that work on a huge turntable at Kent-Johnson headquarters. In the case of Hush, another deodorant for which the partners consented to compose, Kent and Johnson apparently felt they shouldn't even go so far as to knock at the door but contented themselves merely with breathing heavily on it with the slogan, 'Just the w-h-i-s-p-e-r of a cream.'

The approach was not always so modest. 'Some musical commercials need authority,' Johnson would remark. An instance of an authoritative jingle would be that of Quaker Puffed Wheat and Puffed Rice Sparkies. No whispering is permitted in the puffed-wheat field. 'Here comes Quaker w-i-t-h a BANG! BANG!' a Kent-Johnson announcer would bark in the middle of a breakfast-cereal jingle, 'THE WHEAT THAT'S SHOT FROM GUNS!'

Such dramatic interpretations of the explosive nature of the product described were not necessarily conceived overnight. 'We give our clients a hell of a lot of thought,' Kent said. The thought process apparently involved a good deal of what the partners, without defining it further, called 'quonking.'

Kent and Johnson began quonking together in 1939. At that time Johnson had already been in this country a few years, having journeyed over from England at the suggestion of John F. Royal, then a vice-president of NBC, for the purpose of filling up blank sustaining air time on that vast network. Previously, Johnson had been producing a program called 'Soft Lights and Sweet Music' for the British Broadcasting Corporation. At NBC Johnson quickly caused a minor upheaval by putting on the air two artists, Mike Riley and Ed Farley, with a song called 'The Music Goes Round and Round.' The song became such a popular success that Royal sent Johnson the wire, 'THIS BIGGER THAN YES WE HAVE NO BANANAS.'

It was at this stage of Johnson's musical development that he met Kent, a former sporting-goods salesman at Spalding's who in 1931 had orated himself into station WOV and then into NBC as an announcer. At WOV, Kent's duties had included sweeping the studio floors. Between sweeps, he handled the record library of 40 discs (mostly consisting of variations of 'In a Persian Market' and 'In a Monastery Garden'), read out of joke books, and described such news events as could be directly seen from the WOV studio window, for example, a fire in a Loft candy store across the street.

At NBC, with the advent of the remote broadcast, Kent

broadened his range with descriptions of affairs such as the boring of the Lincoln Tunnel and Elks, Moose, and Kiwanis luncheons. Kent later was to feel that this varied experience splendidly prepared him for his eventual entry into the jingle field. The eccentric behavior of an NBC harmonium may also have been a contributing factor. This instrument was used to fill in blank air time and the listening population did not enjoy its reedy quality. It was consequently used only as a last resort, and any announcer who allowed himself to be cut back to the dread harmonium was considered at NBC as inviting unemployment. Under this dire threat, Kent trained himself as he has said, 'so I was never at a loss for a word.'

Kent's education was completed at Mutual, where he produced a program entitled 'Don't You Believe It.' 'We exploded theories,' he told me. This passion for truth must still smolder in Kent. 'Not all fish live under water,' he remarked to me in the course of a conversation. 'There's a fish in Brazil that stays out three hours at a time.'

It was a mutual desire for self-improvement that brought Kent and Johnson together. At their first meeting they did not immediately warm to each other, but fortunately for musical history they shortly reconvened over several Scotches and found themselves in harmony on many questions. One of the subjects on which they agreed most heartily was the lack of taste being shown at the time in radio commercials. As Johnson recalled it the new friends then began to discuss how they might elevate the art of the commercial to a loftier plane — or as Kent recalled it, 'How could we make a buck?'

Whatever the details, the two colleagues quickly evolved the ringing slogan: 'A cake of P and G puts 25 times more soap on the extra dirty spot!' and submitted it to Procter and Gam-

ble, who fairly bubbled with gratitude at this fervent declaration of faith in saponified fats. Kent and Johnson were delighted with their checks; a profitable partnership began.

The two colleagues plunged into further thought and soon emerged with a plan for the master stroke that was to bring the singing commercial into its own, and eventually, to bring about the invention of a device enabling the listener to fade out commercials for a minute at a time. Kent and Johnson took the first few bars of the Cumbrian song 'John Peel,' rearranged them, added a line, 'Nickel, nickel, nickel, nickel,' and converted the whole into a ballad called 'Pepsi-Cola Hits the Spot.'

In composing the Pepsi-Cola jingle, Kent and Johnson incorporated a unique and brilliant feature. After much discussion and experimentation, they designed the jingle to last no more than fifteen seconds, on the theory that it took at least that much time for the average listener to arise from his easy chair and switch off his radio. The Pepsi-Cola jingle, they calculated, would thus beat the listener to the switch. The enormous advantages of this hit-and-run technique were immediately apparent to Walter Mack, then president of the Pepsi-Cola Company, who ordered that the jingle be broadcast day and night across the country.

'Walter Mack was the first man to have the courage of his convictions about the musical commercial,' Johnson remarked gratefully. 'He spent enough money to give it the necessary incidence to really register with the listener.'

The 'incidence' has indeed been considerable. Since 1939, when it was put together, the jingle has been played at least a million times over various radio stations — half a million times in one year alone — and, since the ascendancy of commercial television, frequently over that medium too. For this privilege

Pepsi-Cola has spent at least ten million dollars during the same period. The effervescent ballad has been performed by Pepsi-Cola artists in dozens of languages, including Persian. At one time it was even given commercial distribution through juke boxes in restaurants, drug stores, and taverns throughout the United States, and people paid hundreds of thousands of nickels to hear the tune. And during the Christmas season it was only by sheer strength of will that the administrators of the Empire State Building were able to resist the efforts of Pepsi-Cola representatives to have the jingle chimed over the yuletide carillon of that high edifice.

The enormous commercial success of the Pepsi-Cola jingle, while it was artistically gratifying to Kent and Johnson, occasioned in them slight feelings of remorse. It appears that they made the grievous error of selling the jingle outright to the Pepsi-Cola interests, instead of taking a royalty on its performance. Johnson always insisted to me, however, that the partners' subsequent relations with Pepsi-Cola were cordial. 'Little gestures are constantly passing back and forth,' he told me. One of these little gestures was an urgent summons to the partners, one day, from Mack to drive out to Pepsi-Cola headquarters in Long Island City for an emergency conference. Kent and Johnson rushed out there and were immediately ushered into Mack's private office. They found Mack in a state of deep concern, staring moodily at a little box lying on the large desk in front of him. The composers asked what the trouble was. By way of an answer, Mack reached forward, pressed a lever on the little box, and commanded the partners to listen. The tinkling of a familiar tune emerged from the box. 'It isn't right. This is *not* the Pepsi-Cola jingle!' Mack cried when the tinkling ceased. Becoming more composed, he explained to Kent and Johnson that his company was having thousands of such music boxes made up with the idea of placing them in Pepsi-Cola dispensers so that each time a dispenser poured out a glass of Pepsi-Cola it would also ring out the Pepsi-Cola jingle. 'Something's wrong with the tune, but I don't know what,' he added. 'You men made up this jingle and you ought to know.'

Johnson, electing himself spokesman for the pair, told the soft-drink tycoon that his hunch was correct — the music-box version of the jingle contained an extra note that didn't belong there. 'Okay,' Mack replied unhesitatingly, 'the factory that makes the music boxes is over in Switzerland. You'd better fly there right away and straighten things out.' Johnson, whose schedule didn't allow for such a trip, declined the invitation and ingeniously resolved the problem on the spot. He called for a pair of small pliers and pulled from the drum of the music-box mechanism a tiny pin that had been producing the offending note. The instrument then played the jingle to perfection. Mack was delighted at the solution until the following day, when the partners sent him a bill. In it they evaluated the little consultation at a sum making the cost of a return plane trip to Switzerland seem trifling by comparison.

The extensive promotion of the Pepsi-Cola jingle, while it did not provide Kent and Johnson with continuing royalties, did result in immediate recognition among sponsors of the composers' talents. The partners themselves entered a modest word or two about their availability. 'I can be had — for pelf,' the inviting voice of a Kent-Johnson jingle performer sang out over the radio to prospective advertisers. The pelf was there, and soon it came pouring in. Kent and Johnson were visited by the representatives of antacid kings, rubber barons, and the sovereign rulers of chewing-gum empires. The composers quickly jacked their prices up and took their careful pick of clients, explaining to disappointed prospective sponsors with lesser amounts of money to spend that the pair felt obliged to retain unimpaired their musical standards and their practice of what Johnson would call 'giving the client the benefit of our thinking.' A popping cork here, a BANG! BANG! there — all were thoughtfully designed to repay the sponsor for his interest in the partners' work. Broadcasting transcription tables were turning everywhere with Kent-Johnson compositions such as 'Pillsbury's Pancake Serenade' and 'He's an Old Bulb Snatcher, an Old Bulb-Snatching Man.' Jingles that in earlier periods of their collaboration Kent and Johnson might have scored for accompaniment by banjos or trios they now provided with musical instrumentation of heroic proportions. Thus, for 'Pillsbury's Pancake Serenade,' the two men provided a score calling for twenty-three brass instruments, a Hammond organ, and several male voices. The theme was set in a minor key, with many rich shadings designed to appeal to lady listeners. 'My work is often strongly influenced by Delius,' Johnson once told me. On the whole, however, he has never confined himself to a particular style of musical expression, and few listeners would find recognizable traces of another composer in his chorus written for the Borden Company and scored for, among other instruments, a small set of cowbells:

> *Boy, but she's a wow!*
> *Elsie the glamorous cow*
> *Oh her eyes are dreamy*
> *And her milk is creamy*
> *Boy, but she's a* woww! —

to which a sexy female voice would add: MooooOOO to YouuuuuuUUU!

The composition of such works, the supervision of their recording, and all the attendant negotiations usually kept Kent and Johnson terribly busy, of course, and most of the time their office was the scene of intense activity, with visiting advertising men pacing about the floors, renditions of jingles being pounded out on a grand piano, ice being broken out of the refrigerator for Martinis, and telephones and doorbells ringing incessantly. Above the din, snatches of the partners' conversation could be heard: Johnson's well-modulated voice, coming from the direction of the grand piano, remarking, 'For this one, you want penetration, not irritation . . .'; Kent's, sharper, saying, 'We were dickering with a bunch of independent freezers . . . '; or again, 'After all, we want to shake a man's hand before putting it in his pocket . . .' Periodically, one or the other of the jingle kings would depart for a conference elsewhere in town. For such excursions Johnson, during the colder months of the year, would wear a huge otter-skin coat which he claimed to have had bequeathed to him by an uncle in Alaska, and he drove himself around town in a long Duesenberg. Kent's clothes, too, often had touches of seasonal individualism, and it was a pleasant sight to see him on a mild spring morning descending the steps outside the partners' office wearing yellow gloves and a long coat with an astrakhan collar, on his way to an interview with a vice-president of the New York Telephone Company, to whom he was going to propose replacing some of the company's telephone bells by a set of chimes that, when the phone rang, would sound a series of mellow notes arranged by Kent and Johnson. The partners were always coming up with novel musical ideas, and they once attempted to persuade a high official of the Catholic Church in New York to have what Johnson gravely described as 'a short composition of our devising' played on the carillon of St. Patrick's Cathedral. The dignitary involved is said to have been rather touched at the idea until he became aware that the short composition was to be recorded from a sound track on the street and was intended to be used as part of a jingle for a soap company.

Despite such seeming eccentricities in their approach to their work, Kent and Johnson nevertheless looked over their clients' products with an extremely cool eye before accepting a musical commission, and they were never averse to scanning a mass of market-research statistics about the product involved before plunging into the labors of actual composition. A case in point was the anxiety of the Corn Products Refining Company to feed more of its Mazola Salad Oil to people.

'We were called in to handle the Mazola problem,' Johnson recalled, 'and, by the time we finished, the number of people who could correctly identify it as the Mazola program had risen from 19 per cent to 46 per cent.' The jingle kings accomplished this soothing miracle by the use of a bass player named Bobby Haggart, who 'whistled through his teeth' the lines 'Mazola fries them . . . right on down! (Sharp chorus) MazollAH!' 'The spontaneous screams that went up from the audience at the end of the commercial were most satisfactory to us,' Johnson told me.

Other coups included a talking engine for Esso Gasoline and a song for Mission Bell Wine which, later relyricized, was converted into a best-selling popular tune.

Such musical feats are said to have brought Kent and Johnson, in one year alone and from one sponsor, twenty thousand dollars, and in that same year the pair had twenty-seven sponsors. One reason for this comfortable income was undoubtedly the partners' firm determination, immediately on seeing what Pepsi-Cola did with their jingle, never again to sell their works outright but to collect instead substantial royalties for every single use of them on radio or television. 'They lease it out to you like a telephone line,' one advertising man remarked to me in discussing the Kent-Johnson service. He rather sadly described their contracts as 'hideous' and 'merciless.'

For their part, of course, Kent and Johnson considered their compensation as only just and equitable, and they frequently pointed out to all concerned the rigors of invention to which they were subjected. To reinforce this impression, they sometimes may have gone out of their way to uphold the traditions of musical struggle. I heard of one advertising executive who, after having, one summer day, requested that Kent and Johnson prepare as quickly as possible a jingle for a beer company, telephoned them the next day and told them that he would come over to discuss progress with them. He arrived at Kent-Johnson headquarters to find the composers stripped to the waist with wet towels wrapped round their heads. The pair spent most of the interview scribbling furiously on pieces of paper and declaring that the assignment was virtually impossible to fulfill within the time-limits that had been set. They said, however, that they would work unceasingly through the night in an attempt to satisfy their client. The executive apologized profusely for the trouble he was causing and, as it was described to me, lurched out of the apartment with guilt written all over his face — an unusual visual effect in the advertising profession. After his departure, the composers sat back and relaxed with Scotches and sodas. They had written the entire jingle some eighteen hours previously, and had even had it recorded, complete with chorus and popping corks.

Since I last saw the pair together, Kent has gone off to pursue a couple of special projects of his own, and the partnership has become inactive. But Johnson is still busily composing jingles for beers, toothpastes, detergents, shaving creams, brands of coffee, and the like, and not long ago when I saw him dressed in a Bond Street suit and looking as prosperous as ever, he was hard at work on the problem of incorporating into a musical commercial for a cold tablet company a specially designed sound effect that he described as 'an electronic sneeze.' His new sneeze, he cheerfully assured me, would communicate to radio and television audiences a feeling of misery itself.

NO
Lobster Men
from
Neptune

W hile browsing among the channels of my
television set during the early evening hours of the past few
years, I have found myself picking up from time to time this
or that program for children. Until not too long ago, most of
the programs in this category that I lingered with long enough
to comprehend consisted of marionette shows and old cowboy
movies. As time went on, however, I began to be aware that a
change had taken place in the nature of the visual, not to mention audible, entertainment being offered young America just
before bedtime. A new element was present — space. A vogue
had set in for dramas dealing with interplanetary travel centuries hence, shattering episodes that involved screeching
rockets, crackling ray guns, and plastic-helmeted adventurers.
Because it seemed to me characteristic of the headlong evolu-
tion of television that its programs for children, having galloped
through the classic stages of puppetry and the nickelodeon,
should now bound far into outer space — and into the future
itself — for inspiration, I made up my mind to find out how
one of these cosmic dramas was produced. It turned out to be

a rewarding inquiry, which launched me into a world of secret codes, dinosaur tracks, and DDT bombs, not to mention the new cosmology.

Three major programs tailored along interplanetary-space lines were being broadcast over two of the major television networks — 'Space Patrol,' over the American Broadcasting Company; 'Tom Corbett, Space Cadet,' also over ABC; and 'Captain Video,' over Du Mont. They were all serials. The action in them was supposed to take place in times ranging from the twenty-first century ('Captain Video'), to the thirty-first century ('Space Patrol'). The characters in 'Tom Corbett, Space Cadet' were exploring the solar system of four hundred years from now. Three times a week they soared to other worlds in rocket ships, warded off space pirates, uttered exclamations like 'Great Galaxy!' and 'Blast me for a Martian mouse!' and on occasion, untrammeled by the force of gravity, they gamboled upside down in the heavens themselves. 'Tom Corbett, Space Cadet' seemed futuristic enough for me, so I called up Rockhill Productions, which produced the show, and was put in touch with Allen Ducovny, the man in charge of the program. Television producers are usually glad to oblige reporters and Ducovny, on hearing that I was interested in learning how a typical performance was put together, courteously invited me over to his place of business.

The headquarters of Rockhill Productions are in a small office building on East Fiftieth Street, across from St. Patrick's Cathedral. The entrance to the building is of somber and faintly ecclesiastical design, but the approaches to Rockhill Productions itself, on the ninth floor, are lined with glass brick and glow with modernity. Ducovny, a short, genial man who was wearing a conservative business suit and a conservative striped tie, received me behind this translucent honeycomb in a room with soundproof walls, dim lights, luxurious green leather chairs, and an awesomely hushed atmosphere. In one corner stood a movie projection screen, in the one opposite it a movie projector.

'This is our viewing room,' Ducovny said, after shaking hands. 'We use it for looking over odd bits of film that we are considering showing on "Tom Corbett, Space Cadet" and for viewing kinescopes — motion-picture transcriptions of the program, that is — which we send to affiliated out-of-town stations to broadcast at whatever hours suit them best. We also use this room for story conferences. We'll be having a story conference here shortly — we're working up a new sequence — and I thought you might like to sit in on it. The production boys and I are going to kick around a few ideas with Willy Ley, the rocket man. Willy was one of the founders of the German Rocket Society, and, of course, he's probably the best-known authority today on the subject of space travel. He was PM's rocket expert during the war. He's also a naturalist, and that's a help, too. We've retained him as technical adviser for "Tom Corbett." We try to have the show as scientifically accurate as possible.'

Ducovny paused, possibly in quiet tribute to scientific accuracy. Then he went on to say that 'Tom Corbett, Space Cadet' was being broadcast over about forty television stations affiliated with ABC, that it was sponsored by the Kellogg Company — the manufacturers of, among other things, Corn Flakes and Pep — and that it was a terrific success. I asked how many people tuned in on the television program each week. 'The viewers would run into the astronomical millions,' Ducovny replied.

He waited while I made note of this estimate, and then continued, ' "Tom Corbett" is dedicated to stimulating the interest of the young in the possibility of traveling to other planets, a subject that has interested man as far back as history is recorded. Anything to do with space is fascinating to kids. They've heard about V-2's, they've heard about artificial satellites, they've heard about the plan — a German scientist broke all the papers with it only a short time ago — for traveling to Mars and back in two years and two hundred and thirty-nine days, in easy stages, with way stations established in permanent orbits around the earth and Mars. Kids are space-conscious. "Tom Corbett" appeals to that space-consciousness by combining adventure and the very latest knowledge of the problems likely to be encountered in traveling to other planets. And, thanks to an electronic gismo in the studio control room that our director, George Gould, thought up, we are able to achieve trick effects on the screen, like free falls in space, that were hitherto impossible in television.'

'Tom Corbett, Space Cadet' first went on the air in the autumn of 1950, a little more than a year after the debut of 'Captain Video.' Ducovny indicated that the program was well received right from the start. 'I'm glad to say that we've caught up with "Video," rating-wise, and even nose them out once in a while,' he told me. 'In fact, nowadays we're even taking the play away from cowboy movies. Horse-opera is definitely slipping on television. Still strong, I admit, but slipping. These kid shows tend to go in cycles. Horse-opera took the play away from puppets on television. Puppets took the play away from "Superman" on radio, and "Superman" took it away from the "Jack Armstrong, All-American Boy" and "Renfrew of the Mounted" type of radio show.'

72

I asked where 'Buck Rogers,' a radio program I recalled hearing in prewar times that also involved space travel, fitted into the picture.

'I'd say "Superman" took the play away from "Buck Rogers," too,' Ducovny replied. ' "Rogers" began on radio in 1932, and it had a pretty long run. Kellogg had it, Cocomalt had it, Cream of Wheat had it, and General Foods had it. I'd say the peak of its success came between 1933 and 1935, when Cocomalt had it. "Rogers" tailed off during the war, I believe. Peter Paul candy tried to revive it for television on ABC in '49, but they let it go after a little while. One of the big troubles that kind of program finds itself facing is that in the last few years youngsters have become pretty well aware of what science can do and what it can't do, so they're fairly critical on technical grounds of electronic razzle-dazzle in stories. "Buck Rogers" went in heavily for disintegrator-ray guns and mad scientists. Kids will accept only so much of that nowadays.'

The debut of 'Superman' on radio, in 1938, probably marked the first successful departure from the 'Buck Rogers' tradition of electromechanical wizardry in the field of interplanetary adventure, Ducovny told me. Ducovny himself was the director of 'Superman' for a while in the early 'forties. One of the principal theories back of 'Superman,' he said, was that while sophisticated young listeners would probably feel that miracle-producing gadgets have little scientific validity, they might be willing to accept miracles made possible by the superhuman characteristic of the hero himself; thus, children might tend to question the scientific feasibility of, say, an airplane that could fly through walls but be willing to accept the idea of a Superman resilient enough to swoop unscathed through a concrete abutment eight feet thick.

' "Superman" was a big success on radio,' Ducovny said. 'The Blue Network had tied up the five-to-six-o'clock block with adventure shows, and was trying to corner the kid market. "Superman" stood alone on Mutual at five-fifteen, the only kid show in the late-afternoon Mutual block. As soon as Superman went on the air, he began taking the play away from Blue. Superman provided security for kids. He was omnipotent. He was indestructible. He could move planets out of their orbits. He had X-ray vision. He could travel faster than the speed of sound. Hell, he could telephone from New York to Los Angeles, bound over to L.A. ahead of the electrical impulse carrying his voice, and talk to himself long distance. The program developed such a pull that other shows began falling in line with the idea. Even Tom Mix went in for Superman-type adventures on the air for a time.'

'Superman' did fairly well on the radio during the war, according to Ducovny, despite the fact that Superman himself had to be classified 4-F in case young listeners should start to wonder why he didn't whip the enemy singlehanded. The writers of the show accomplished this by having Superman flunk his Army physical by turning on his X-ray vision during the eye examination, with the result that he read off the letters on the sight-test chart in the next room instead of on the one he was supposed to be looking at. Superman's strength, I gathered, proved to be his weakness in more ways than one. 'Superman was great, but the difficulty was that we couldn't dream up antagonists worthy of him,' Ducovny said. 'Being as all-powerful as he was, no villain stood a chance of doing him in. Dramatically, he tended to lose momentum. He had no Achilles' heel.'

Eventually, Ducovny said, the writers of the program decided that they would simply *have* to provide Superman with an Achilles' heel, and so they devised one — a near-fatal allergy to kryptonite, a substance capable of robbing even Superman of his strength. The enervating stuff was inserted into the script shortly after the end of the war. The writers, in the interests of topicality, made kryptonite radioactive and unstable and placed it in the hands of a Dr. Teufel, an equally unstable German scientist who was out to rule the world, and Superman, too. Ingenious as these touches were, though, the Achilles' heel represented, at best, a combination of the old stratagems of the disintegrator ray and the mad scientist and, according to

Ducovny, could not be expected to restore a great deal of Superman's momentum. Superman went off radio in 1949 — hoist, it would seem, with his own petard.

In the manner of a man who has learned his lesson well, Ducovny went on to explain how 'Tom Corbett, Space Cadet' differed from its predecessors. 'The basic appeal of "Tom Corbett" is its realism,' he said. 'Our stories are not in the realm of fantasy. The action is within the limits of physical possibility. It has believability. No disintegrator rays. No mad scientists. No lobster men from Neptune. It is our policy to show the process of interplanetary travel, and the conditions on the planets we travel to, as accurately as science can today.'

A young, athletic-looking man entered the room. He was in shirtsleeves and appeared, from his well-loosened collar and tie, to have been undergoing a strenuous period of creative effort. Ducovny introduced him as Albert Aley, the script editor of 'Tom Corbett, Space Cadet,' and, after telling him the purpose of my visit, suggested that he try to outline the dramatic structure of the program for me.

After some thought, Aley said, 'Put Frank Merriwell in a space suit and throw in "The Three Musketeers," and you'd be getting at the general idea. Merriwell and his sidekicks operated out of Yale. Corbett and *his* sidekicks operate out of the Space-port, at Space Academy, four hundred years ahead of the present. Space Academy is the West Point of the Universe. The Universe is at peace four hundred years ahead of the present. Space Academy is the instrument of the Solar Guard, the peace-enforcement unit of the Solar Alliance. Earth people

have colonized Mars, Venus, and Titan, a satellite of Saturn. Tom Corbett, along with two other Space Cadets and an officer of the Solar Guard, takes off in his rocket-powered space ship, the *Polaris*, to maintain peace on the colonized planets and to explore the possibility of colonizing others.'

'The concept of peace is one that parents approve of,' Ducovny said.

'No gore in this show,' Aley said. 'The only complaint we've had was when a stranger made his way to Earth from the planet Alcar. He wore fairly sinister makeup and perhaps he did look a little frightening. A few mothers wrote in words of gentle admonition, and we toned down the Alcarian's makeup right away. We lay off horror. So far, we've had only one death on the show, and that was accidental.' This death occurred during a small-scale war on the planet Mercury, the twilight, or habitable, zone of which the Space Cadets were considering colonizing. 'It wasn't even a war. More like a skirmish, come to think of it,' Aley said. 'The Mercurians had misinterpreted an inspection visit by the Space Cadets, and thought it was an invasion. In the scuffle that followed, one of the Mercurians collapsed and died, but we managed to patch up the trouble, and there have since been no untoward incidents on Mercury. We had a revolution on Mars, and we patched that up, too. The Martian commander was stealing the fuel of rocket ships belonging to other members of the Solar Alliance, hoping to build up a fuel monopoly for aggressive purposes. He was a Martian nationalist, the bastard. We broke up the plot and let him escape to an asteroid.'

Aley said that it was Willy Ley who had given the writers the idea of dispatching the Martian troublemaker to this bleak place of exile. 'Willy has been enormously helpful to us,' he went on. 'For example, the writers wanted to make a space-opera sequence out of the old horse-opera deal in which a moss-back prospector finds a gold pile and later gets double-crossed by his partners. The writers wanted this fellow to stake a claim to some precious mineral in space. Willy suggested that they have him discover an asteroid of nearly pure gold. Then they wanted a scientific way of handling the double-cross by the space prospector's partners. Willy solved that one by having the double-crossers push the asteroid out of its orbit with the nose of their rocket ship and substitute a worthless asteroid in the orbit. The payoff came when the golden asteroid went into an elliptical orbit around the sun and got too hot for the double-crossers to handle.'

Ducovny remarked that the writers never attempted to insert into the program any action that Ley felt to be outside the limits of scientific possibility. 'If the boys are thinking of flying through the tail of a comet, they check with Willy to make sure that it's possible to do so without serious damage to the rocket ship by stellar debris,' Ducovny said.

At this point, Ley, a short, broad-shouldered man, entered the room, wearing a blue suit, and a blue tie on which was printed, in another shade of blue, the outline of a rocket. 'I've just been downtown to check the layout on those models of Space Academy that Marx toys are putting on the market,' he said to Ducovny. 'The takeoff area seems to be pretty much in line with the design I roughed out.'

After being introduced to Ley, I told him that we had been discussing his advice to the writers about stellar debris. 'Ah, yes, space junk,' he said. 'The writers are always wanting their ship to *hit* something out in space. Thank God I've got them to stop hitting asteroids for a while. The probabilities of

79

a space ship's encountering an asteroid in its path, you know, are so slight as to be negligible. The writers were overdoing it. They wanted to hit an asteroid practically every week. "Please, boys," I told them. "Only once or twice a year." '

I confessed to Ley that I didn't know much about rockets aside from the sort of thing I'd seen on television, and I asked him what kind of progress American rocket research was making toward interplanetary flight.

'Tremendous progress,' Ley replied. 'Today we have an altitude record of a hundred and thirty-five miles by a so-called single-stage rocket, the Viking. And we have the two-hundred-and-fifty-mile altitude record by the two-stage rocket built for Army Ordnance. In the imminent future, we can expect, without the development of any essentially new design, an orbital rocket — a three-stage job whose final component would leave the earth's atmosphere and circle the earth like a satellite. Within a comparatively few years, we should be able to send an unmanned rocket to the moon in ninety-seven hours, but it would have to crash there. Manned rockets are considerably farther off in time. The action in "Tom Corbett" is set four hundred years in the future. Nevertheless, I have said repeatedly, and still say, that the manned interplanetary rocket will be a reality within only *two* hundred years.'

Ley's predictions were cut short by the arrival of the writers — Willie Gilbert, a short, pleasant-looking man, and Jack Weinstock, a man of medium height, with a calm and authoritative manner. 'Willie Gilbert works pretty much full time on our scripts,' Ducovny told me. 'Jack has a lot of other work to do, being a doctor with a large and lucrative practice.'

This combination of literary and medical skills struck me

as unusual. I said so. Dr. Weinstock assured me that the explanation was simple. 'I specialize in urology,' he said. 'I've also been a general practitioner, and I'm now house doctor for several of the Shubert theaters, backstage and up front — that is, I'm on call during performances. I've been writing little things on and off for years. Occasionally, I would get off bits of dialogue, and so on, for theatrical people who happened to be patients of mine, but I didn't start to write professionally until after I ran into Willie Gilbert. That was in 1946.'

'We met when Jack was about to deliver my wife's baby,' Gilbert said. 'I was pacing the corridors in the hospital. Jack came out to calm me down. We talked, then met again and talked some more. We discovered that we were both involved in show business. I had my own vaudeville act at one time. It was called "The Micromaniacs." Satirical comedy. As I say, Jack and I kicked the gong around.'

'That's right,' Dr. Weinstock said. 'And as a result, we began to bang things out. We wrote a satirical ballet number for *Tickets, Please!* and a raft of other things. We've sold practically everything we've written so far. None of this struggling-author stuff.' He added that he and Gilbert had submitted their first 'Tom Corbett, Space Cadet' script to Rockhill Productions about a year ago, and that they had been at it ever since.

'The boys made a hit from the beginning,' Ducovny said. 'Originally, we had five or six writers working on "Tom Corbett." Then Willie and Jack came in — collaborating with the others at the start and gradually taking over the whole job. For one of their first scripts, Jack invented a disease called space fever — it occurs when a space traveler is subjected to fluctuating pressures — and had it appear that one of the characters in the show was about to come down with it. That script jumped our audience rating several points.'

I asked Dr. Weinstock if he would summarize the symptoms of space fever for me. 'Low threshold of irritability, vertigo, and passing out at critical moments,' he said.

'And Jack gave one of the boys anoxemia on the moon,' Gilbert said. 'Anoxemia is an illness caused by lack of oxygen. It made a swell sequence.'

I asked Dr. Weinstock how he managed all this celestial medical activity in addition to his earthly practice. 'It isn't easy,' he said. 'We usually work week ends, and sometimes week nights, too. Willie even comes up and waits outside the operating room till we can put in a few minutes together. Most of my patients don't connect me with television, even though my name appears in the program credit. In the waiting room of my office one day, I heard a mother tell her boy that if he behaved himself there, she'd let him watch "Tom Corbett" that night. I didn't mention to her that I had anything to do with the show.'

Dr. Weinstock and Gilbert excused themselves then and went into a huddle over some technical matters, and Ducovny told me that the production conference would begin as soon as Gould, the director, arrived. The purpose of the conference, he said, was to establish the basic setting for a new sequence, which was to run for about four weeks. At preliminary talks on the matter, Aley, the writers, and Ducovny had come to the conclusion that what Tom Corbett needed was a change of scene from his usual planetary rounds. 'The writers agreed that we were temporarily up against a blank wall,' Ducovny said. 'We'd been to Venus, we'd been to Mars, we'd been to Mercury — the twilight zone of it, anyhow — and we'd been to

Saturn and to Titan. We were afraid of getting repetitious. We wanted to get out on a new planet. Al Aley brought forward the idea that maybe we ought to go right out of our own solar system and away into outer space. We asked Willy Ley what he thought of the idea. He applauded it. We asked him what we could expect out there. He said we could expect other solar systems. We continued the discussion, and out of it came the theory that there might be planets pretty much like our own — even one resembling Earth in its prehistoric stage of development.'

'We thought that might be a good way of working in some prehistoric animals,' Aley said. 'We once had a Venutian worm on one of our shows, and it attracted a lot of interest. Anyway, we're agreed on sending Tom Corbett on a trip of exploration to some new planet a hundred million years behind Earth, evolution-wise, and still in an age when dinosaurs roam.'

A few minutes later, Gould arrived, and the conference got under way. Ducovny opened the proceedings by stating that, for the forthcoming sequence, he thought he could get some trick motion-picture film from Hollywood of dinosaurs in action. Then, turning to Ley, he asked whether he could suggest a likely astronomical setting for the kind of planet they had in mind.

'Modern astronomy generally accepts the theory that most stars of the main, or hydrogen-helium, sequence have planets, and we have approximately seven billion main-sequence stars in our galaxy alone,' Ley said. 'According to the law of probability, there *ought* to be something out there along the lines you want. I suggest you place it within the solar system of Alpha Centauri, which is comparatively close to our own solar system. Alpha Centauri is a main-sequence star of about the size of our sun, and it's roughly twenty-four thousand billion miles away.'

The suggestion appeared acceptable to everybody.

'Willy will triangulate the position of the planet for you later,' Aley told the writers.

'The way we see it,' Dr. Weinstock said to Ley, 'the take-off from Space Academy will be pretty routine. No accidents this time.'

'Good enough,' Ley replied. 'Don't forget to switch the artificial-gravity generator on *after* the blast-off, not before. You don't want to subject your men to the force of Earth gravity and artificial gravity at the same time. As a matter of fact, a thirty-foot-a-second take-off acceleration happens in itself to be a sufficient substitute for Earth gravity.'

'Anything special in the way of supplies?' Gilbert asked.

'Apart from the usual oxygen masks, and so on, I suggest you provide the crew with a good supply of pemmican,' Ley said. 'Cakes of soap will do the trick. They look like the real thing. Incidentally, I wouldn't use food pills. Some other space show has been feeding its crew food pills, and anyway they couldn't possibly work. The average man needs at least two pounds of starches and proteins per twenty-four-hour period.'

Gould, who had apparently been deep in thought, turned to Ley and asked, 'How far is this Alpha Centauri, again?'

'Four and a third light-years,' Ley told him.

'I was just wondering — isn't it true that the speed of light is the fastest you can go, even theoretically?' Gould asked.

'That theory has been punctured time and again, and is self-contradictory,' Ley replied. After a moment of reflection, he went on, 'We'll be obliged to take some liberties with the time factor, of course. Maybe the best way to handle the prob-

84

lem of just how long it would take to reach the planet would be to pretty much ignore the time factor. We could just equip the space ship with something we might call Hyper-drive, and let it go at that.'

The writers seemed quite willing to let the Hyper-drive dispose of the time factor, and the discussion turned to the question of what sights, apart from dinosaurs, Tom Corbett and his companions might be expected to encounter on the new planet. Ley said they could expect a rugged terrain of sheer cliffs, thick jungles, and mud flats, and perhaps occasional geysers of methane gas.

'But what other *monsters* could we use?' Ducovny wanted to know.

'The dominant forms of life in the Mesozoic Age on Earth, a hundred million years ago, were reptilian,' Ley said. 'Mammals did exist, but most of them were small marsupials. There were birds, too, but I think you'd better concentrate on reptiles.'

'I know where I can get my hands on some salamanders,' Gould said. 'Would they be all right?'

'Salamanders are amphibians, not reptiles,' Ley told him. 'Their young breathe water. And I'm afraid their legs wouldn't resemble anything in the Mesozoic Age.'

'Is there anything around these days that looks like a pterodactyl, maybe?' Gould asked.

'I'm afraid not,' Ley said.

'How about a bat?' Dr. Weinstock suggested.

'Entirely different wing structure,' Ley said.

'Could we use snakes?' Aley asked.

'Snakes are a comparatively recent evolutionary development,' Ley said. He gazed thoughtfully around the room, and

85

then added, 'You could always try to get a hatteria, a type of which existed in the Mesozoic and still exists today. You'd have to get it from New Zealand, though, and they're heavily protected there. Or you might get a Gila monster, in which case, of course, you'd have to arrange to have it defanged.'

'Well, gee,' said Ducovny, looking worried.

'Maybe we could get something from the zoo,' Gould said.

'You might be able to get a turtle,' Ley said. 'A type of giant turtle existed in the Mesozoic.'

'A turtle would be swell,' Ducovny said, brightening up.

'Also, you might try to find yourself a nice crocodile,' Ley said. 'The modern crocodile, after all, is related to the Mesozoic teleosaur.'

'That *sounds* O.K., Willy,' Ducovny said doubtfully. 'The only difficulty there is that we want action in the show, and, frankly, most of the crocodiles I've seen at the zoo don't seem to do anything but just lie around. How could you get a crocodile to open his mouth on cue?'

'Dangle a fresh piece of beef in front of him, just out of camera range,' Ley said.

A few days later, Ducovny called me up and invited me to the camera rehearsal — the equivalent of a dress rehearsal in the theater — of one of the episodes that had grown out of these deliberations. On my way over to it, I stopped in to see Hal Davis, a vice-president of Kenyon & Eckhardt, one of the advertising agencies that represent the far-flung interests of the Kellogg Corporation. Davis, Ducovny had told me, was the man who 'promoted' the 'Tom Corbett, Space Cadet' program. As I was not altogether sure of just what promoting a program involves, I thought I might as well find out from Davis himself.

It involves several things, as I began learning a minute or

so after Davis, a round-faced man of robustly cheerful appearance, received me in his office. I had scarcely sat down when he opened a drawer of his desk and pulled out and identified for me a Space Cadet Planet Guide, a Space Cadet Rocket Ring, a Space Cadet Army Badge, a Space Cadet Squadron Cloth Arm Patch, a Space Cadet Magic Moving-Picture Eye Take-off Viewer, a Universal Space Pledge Certificate, a deed to an unspecified area of the moon's surface, and a phonograph record of 'The Space Cadet Song and March,' by the Space Cadet Chorus and Orchestra.

'Just a few of our promotional gimmicks,' Davis said when I had finished examining these items. 'Some of them we put in the Space Kit, a twenty-five-cent self-liquidating Kellogg box-top premium. Most premiums are self-liquidating, you know. The asking price just covers the cost of producing and handling. Some of the gimmicks, like the Space Cadet Rings, we give away in packages of cereal. We've got the green light from the Kellogg people on "Tom Corbett." What a sales medium! Do you know that even before this program came along the sale of Kellogg's Corn Flakes and Kellogg's Pep together represented about 25 per cent of all dry-cereal sales in the country? When you've got a product moving on that scale, it's almost impossible to get any program to make an impact on sales, but "Corbett" has done just that. In fact, it's raised Pep and Corn Flakes sales 100 per cent in certain areas. The client is hot. The Kellogg people feel that "Corbett" is the best sales vehicle in the cereal market ever — bigger even than their "Howdy Doody." "Howdy Doody" has Rice Crispies. "Corbett" has Pep and Corn Flakes.'

I asked Davis how his promotional efforts had been received by the public. 'Nicely, nicely,' he said. 'A while ago, we worked out a deal with the Hayden Planetarium by which we built them an Interplanetary Spaceport exhibit where people could make reservations for travel to the moon, and all. We also hope to fix up a display at the Planetarium showing how people will buy their cereal four hundred years from now. We've come up with something called Spin and Eat, which is a bowl with Pep, milk, sugar, and dehydrated fruit wrapped in separate membranes — cellophane ones that in four hundred years would be replaced by some substance that could be consumed with the cereal. You spin the spoon on top of the bowl and that breaks the membranes and mixes the ingredients. We've also been working with the United Nations publicity guys on an idea for getting kids together from all over — children of delegates — to talk about space travel, and the world being at peace, and all. We haven't figured out all the angles yet, but the *Herald Tribune* likes the U.N., and since they run the "Space Cadet" comic strip, they ought to work along with us. Then we're working on the possibility of having Kellogg salesmen wear Space Cadet uniforms when they call on grocery stores, which could be an angle. A little while ago, we arranged to present a special flag to the Air Cadet League of Canada, to be taken to the moon when the first Canadian airman lands there. That angle worked out nicely — lots of publicity. We had the flag made of nylon, and had it backed with stiff material, so it wouldn't hang limp. There's no wind on the moon, according to Willy Ley.'

Davis went on to say that 'Tom Corbett, Space Cadet' received a big boost during the previous Christmas-shopping season, when Gimbel's devoted a window to a replica of Tom Corbett's space ship, the *Polaris*. 'Gimbel's had twenty-three Space Cadet items on sale throughout the store,' Davis said. 'It was a

Space Cadet Christmas. We had another space ship — a huge one — made up for the toy section, and the kids could go inside the thing and see what it was like to take a trip to the moon. We had different characters from the TV show turn up for autographs and general stuff. Six thousand kids went through the space ship on the day it opened, and we arranged for Gimbel's to give away a hundred thousand Space Cadet rings and a hundred and twenty-five thousand boxes of Pep during the Christmas season. Gimbel's sold a lot of our Space Kits, too. Normally, you have to turn in a box top to get one, but in this case the kids could buy the kits *without* the box tops, so long as they pledged themselves to eat better breakfasts.'

Davis handed me a partial list of Space Cadet merchandise. The items on it numbered around fifty and included, in addition to the paraphernalia he had already shown me, the Space Cadet Strat-O-Phone (a kind of walkie-talkie), the Space Cadet tie (it glows in daylight), the Space Cadet crash helmet, Space Cadet suspenders, and the Space Cadet rocket ship. 'The rocket ship runs along the floor and shoots red and green sparks from its exhaust,' Davis said. 'It's very realistic. Willy Ley acts as scientific adviser on the design of a lot of our Tom Corbett merchandise, as well as for the show. By the way, did I give you the Tom Corbett Space Cadet Secret Code chart? We're beginning to get letters from kids written in the Tom Corbett code.'

The broadcasts of the 'Tom Corbett, Space Cadet' program were originating in a studio on the top floor of a building on West Fifty-seventh Street. A victim of Davis's generosity, I arrived at the building to attend the camera rehearsal laden down with Space Cadet planet guides, take-off viewers, and rocket rings, and met Ducovny in the hallway on the ground floor, where he was supervising the arrival of some canvas flats for scenery. It required several elevator trips to get them all up to the studio, and while we were waiting, Ducovny told me that earlier that day the actors had gone through their preliminary paces in the auditorium of the Village Presbyterian Church, on West Thirteenth Street. Television producers, he explained, are plagued by a lack of space for rehearsals, and this shortage had obliged Rockhill to turn to the ministry for help in housing the 'Tom Corbett, Space Cadet' preliminary runs. As for the finished performances that go out on the air, and dress rehearsals of them, such as the one I was going to see upstairs, he said, ABC had been fortunate in being able to lease, on a part-time basis, studio facilities owned by an organization that trains people to be broadcasters.

'ABC has several kinescope duplicates made of each episode of "Tom Corbett" to take care of out-of-town distribution,' Ducovny said. ' "Corbett" goes on the air at six-thirty in the New York area — parents let their kids view television considerably beyond the five-to-six block usual on radio, you know — but other stations, farther west, where the time is different, don't want it that early, and that's where kinescopes come in. Kinescopes are pretty expensive, so we bicycle the prints to them. "Bicycling" is a term that originated in the nickelodeon days, when one film print traveled right around the circuit, being rushed from one movie house to another by bike messenger. ABC usually bicycles our kinescopes by Air Express.'

The last of the scenery had been dispatched, and Ducovny and I took the elevator up to the studio, a large room with a great clutter of lights and scaffolding overhead, under which cameras were being wheeled around on dollies, long microphone booms were waving about in the air like oversized fishing poles, and stagehands were rushing this way and that, all to the accompaniment of a great deal of hammering. In the center of the room artificial jungle vines hung from a scaffolding near the ceiling and spread along the floor. No actors were in sight, but I spotted Gould standing deep in the interior of the jungle. He emerged after a moment and began dispersing with a few kicks a number of rocks — made of cork, I supposed, from the way they tumbled around — that a stagehand was emptying from a big carton. In front of the vines, in the middle of a more careful arrangement of rocks, the outline of a large reptilian footprint had been painted on the floor. At one side of the room stood a model — about twenty feet high, made of plywood, canvas, and cardboard, and painted gray — of the fins, the jet exhausts, and what appeared to be the tail entrance of a rocket ship. Across the room stood another model, this one of the pilot's compartment at the nose end of the ship.

Ducovny had hurried over to a man in overalls who was standing at a table near the pilot's compartment. I went to join them, stepping over coaxial cables that twisted everywhere, like exposed roots of trees.

'I tried Farina earlier, but it was too lumpy,' I heard the man in overalls say to Ducovny as I approached.

Looking over Ducovny's shoulder, I saw on the table a shallow tray. It was filled with a pale-brown gelatinous substance, and a half-empty box of Wheatena stood next to it.

'This guy is one of our prop men,' Ducovny explained to me, 'and the stuff in that tray is the mud flat Willy Ley suggested we find on the planet. Wheatena.' He then asked the prop man whether the cereal had cooled off. The prop man said it had. 'Very well,' Ducovny said. 'The turtle, please.'

The prop man picked up a tin box and extracted from it a turtle about two inches long, its head, legs, and tail all drawn up into its shell. I said that it seemed a bit on the small side for a Mesozoic specimen. 'Oh, we'll just shoot him in a close close-up and blow him up to any size we want,' Ducovny assured me, and said to the prop man, 'Put him in.'

The prop man placed the turtle on the surface of the cereal. The turtle extended its head from the shell and, after a languid glance at its surroundings, burrowed into the Wheatena and disappeared. 'Fish him out!' Ducovny cried.

While the turtle was being recovered, Ducovny moved on to another table and inspected a miniature set representing rocks surrounded by foliage. This, he told me, was the lair of the crocodile recommended by Ley. In a moment I spotted the crocodile, a three-inch Mississippi alligator, lying peacefully on a paper rock basking in the rays of several klieg spotlights. The alligator was evidently about to be given the close close-up treatment by a television camera that had been dollied up to within six inches of its jaws. 'O.K., Joe. Let's see your teeth,' a cameraman said coolly to the reptile as he adjusted his focus. Ducovny asked another prop man whether the animal had been showing any signs of life. 'Sometimes he blinks his eyes, sometimes not,' the prop man said. 'Sometimes he moves, sometimes he freezes. I don't know that you can depend on him.'

This news seemed to disconcert Ducovny. 'Maybe we'll have to try a salamander, after all,' he said to me. 'I know its legs aren't right, but it might turn out to be a hell of a lot friskier. Gee, we want *action!*'

I asked Ducovny whether he had managed to obtain the dinosaur motion-picture film. He said that he hadn't, and that instead he had ordered several small plaster models of dinosaurs from a prop-rental shop.

I remarked that I didn't see how he could expect much action from plaster dinosaurs, and he said, 'Lack of action is no problem in their case, I'm happy to say. You see, we've just rearranged the script so that when the dinosaurs come on the screen, they'll appear to have been frozen in their tracks by the boys' Paralo-Ray guns.'

'Ray guns?' I said, surprised. 'I thought you didn't use rays.'

'We don't use *disintegrator* rays,' Ducovny said. 'Paralo-Rays are different. They don't disintegrate anything — they just paralyze.'

Ducovny then took me on a tour of the studio to examine some of the other props. These included a dirty tennis ball, which, suspended from an easel by a thread, would represent a planet; an old Edison Voicewriter with a roll of paper in it, which would represent an electronic machine at Space Academy that automatically types out oral reports relayed to it from space by radio; and a pile of switches and magnetic coils, handily mounted, Ducovny explained, for ready attachment to anything around the studio that might need an extra electronic touch. Stopping beside a small model of a rocket ship, Ducovny showed me a DDT bomb concealed behind it. 'We use this model for shooting take-offs and landings,' he said. 'You get a swell white blast from the DDT bomb that looks like the real thing. Once we tried out a perfume bomb for a take-off scene, because it had a nice dense spray, but the actors yelled blue murder and we had to go back to DDT. And DDT doesn't smell too good, either.'

We moved behind the scenes, and Ducovny showed me a Space Cadet dress uniform, which was a heavily padded, blue-gray affair lavishly embellished with brass studs, and a pressurized Space Suit, which was a pair of cerise-colored, balloon-like coveralls topped by a large Plexiglas dome and a spiral antenna. 'We won't be using the Space Suits today,' he said. 'The boys have landed on the Alpha Centauri planet, and the atmosphere is breathable except for a little methane gas here and there.'

Returning to the set, we passed the model of the pilot's compartment, or, more accurately, of the space ship's control deck. Ducovny pointed out its essential features — gravity generator, cutout relay, hatch leading to the radar bridge, and hatch to the power deck — and went on to say that while this particular prop normally represented the control deck of the *Polaris*, it was also used, on occasion, to represent the control deck of the *Orion*, a sister space ship, whose passengers sometimes include the only female character on the program, Dr. Joan Dale, Doctor of Space Medicine at Space Academy. I asked him whether any romantic entanglement between Dr. Dale and Tom Corbett or some other member of the Corps was permitted in the plot, and his reply made it clear that sex has no place in space-opera. As the cowboy movie hero is sometimes allowed to kiss, in unobtrusive fashion, the nose of his horse, so the hero of the space program may once in a while pat the nose of his rocket ship, and even refer to it affectionately as 'old girl,' but that is as far as things are allowed to go in that direction.

The actors had now arrived. Ducovny introduced them — Frankie Thomas, Al Markim, Jan Merlin, and Ed Bryce. As

94

usual, Thomas was to be Tom Corbett, and the rest were to be his co-adventurers. No Dr. Dale today.

Thomas, like the others, was dressed in light-gray Space Cadet fatigues. He also wore a wide leather belt to which were attached an oven thermometer, a five-inch-long metal tube, an underwater swimming mask, a soldering iron with a transparent Lucite muzzle and with spiral springs decorating its barrel, and a miniature hammer, like the ones used to break the glass of fire-alarm boxes. Aside from the hammer, the significance of which, I discovered, nobody connected with the program could explain, these accoutrements represented, respectively, a Geiger counter, an electroscopic magnifier, an oxygen mask, and a Paralo-Ray gun.

It appeared that the actors had been having trouble with the Paralo-Ray gun. 'Couldn't we have lanyards, like M.P.'s, to secure our guns?' Thomas asked Ducovny. 'They're liable to fall out of the holsters when we're in action. These Lucite muzzles are always dropping off the barrels, too.'

'We'll get you new guns,' Ducovny said indulgently.

Appeased, the actors walked off and began their rehearsal. The Mesozoic explorations of Tom Corbett and his crew were evidently beginning to bear fruit. The actors crouched around the big footprint painted on the floor.

'Great rings of Saturn!' one of them exclaimed. 'What do you make of it, Tom?'

'Looks like a footprint to me,' Tom Corbett said.

With that, a roar of wild beasts burst from the loudspeaker overhead.

'Great Jupiter!' another Space Cadet cried, jerking his soldering iron from its holster and aiming it. As he aimed, a

95

series of ominous crackling and buzzing sounds rose above the din from the loudspeaker, and then the roars died away.

'Great Galaxy! A dinosaur!' Tom Corbett said, peering into the jungle. 'Thank Jupiter those Paralo-Rays took effect!'

'O.K., folks, commercial,' Gould's voice said over the loudspeaker.

An announcer launched into a talk about better ways of building up 'more punch 'til lunch.' When he was through, the loudspeaker began emitting the sound of twittering tropical birds.

I spotted the sound booth near the top of a spiral staircase and made my way up there. The sound man, sitting by his spinning turntables, was eating an apple. With his permission, I looked at the labels of some of the sound-effect records used on the program from time to time. These included 'Earthquakes and Avalanches,' 'Explosions, Single and Multiple,' 'Herd of Elephants Trumpeting,' 'Hippopotamus Calling Mate,' 'Grimalkin Cat,' 'Two Leopards Snarling,' and 'One Dog Howling.' There was also a musical recording entitled simply 'Ghostly-Romantic.'

I returned to the studio just as Gould's voice came over the loudspeaker saying, 'Quiet, please! Let's have the camera on that dinosaur again.'

'Yes, *sir*,' one of the cameramen said, and swiveled across the floor on his dolly toward one of the models.

'No, no!' Gould said sharply. 'Not *that* dinosaur! The one with the long neck — the brontosaur!'

'Jeez, there are so damn *many* monsters here today,' the cameraman said softly as he wheeled around and started toward another miniature set.

Now the cast was ranged in front of a black curtain as if

ready for action. A six-foot ladder, draped in black, stood near by. Tom Corbett climbed the ladder, paused for a moment at the top, and jumped to the floor. I asked Ducovny what this activity was supposed to represent. 'To tell you the truth, in this kind of trick setup the actors *themselves* often don't quite know what they're doing until they see the kinescopes of the actual performance afterward,' he said. 'In this case, Tom Corbett happens to be jumping down from the paralyzed dinosaur's back. You see, we just dub in the dinosaur from another camera, with that electronic gismo I was telling you about.'

'All right, folks, on to the mud flats!' Gould called over the loudspeaker. 'Where's that giant turtle?'

'He's lost himself in the porridge again,' a prop man said, groping glumly in the Wheatena with a spoon.

Wired

for

Sentiment

At the tribal meetings of certain primitive societies the presiding chief was supposed to determine the prevailing mood of opinion by listening to the approving or disapproving clamor of drums set up by attending elders. Nowadays, in the United States, the same sort of process has refined itself into the science and profession of public-opinion measurement. The drums have given way to IBM machines, flashing control panels of electronic calculators, and small armies of Ph.D's from the headquarters of Dr. George Gallup and his colleagues.

Just how many commercial opinion polling companies exist in the United States I cannot say — the statistical business has a remarkable shortage of statistics about itself. But there is no doubt that polling has become a fairly big business. In addition to the big independent pollsters like George Gallup and Elmo Roper, probably 30 per cent of larger corporations, and almost every advertising agency, maintain opinion research staffs.

Although opinion polling as a science is comparatively new, the mathematical process of sampling upon which it is based is by no means so. As early as the time of the American Civil War, the Department of Agriculture found that by having its agents poke around in potato sacks in a small number of scattered American farms and report their findings, it could estimate with fair accuracy potato crop yields over a large area.

In the eighteenth century a Swiss mathematician named Jacob Bernoulli found, after experimenting interminably with bowls full of black and white balls, that by picking a few balls at random from a bowl he could assess within a small predictable margin of error the exact proportion of white to black balls in the entire bowl. Bernoulli's formulation of the Laws of Probability and of Large Numbers became an important part of the basis of sampling procedures vitally useful in every industry today — blood samples in medicine, rock cores in geology, dirt samples in agriculture, water supply in public health, production control in manufacturing, clothing sizes in the garment industry, and so on.

By the 'twenties, the successes of the sampling method in industry inspired the researchers with the new idea of applying Bernoulli's equations to the mass behavior of the human mind, and now we have polling organizations by the score frantically sampling, rating, and predicting public tastes in everything from politics to toothpastes, linoleum, chewing gum, and ideas.

The contributions of the pollsters to the American way of life, while substantial, are not always readily visible, and audiences are often unaware of the scientific graphs and charts that may determine the form, content, and probable effect of what they may read or hear. Yet the science has now advanced to a point where the National Association of Manufactures can hand a draft of an adult 'comic' book dramatizing the American

Way over to a polling organization and be told, to the last decimal point, what its 'depth penetration' into the public mind will be. The drawings can then be suitably altered — possibly a more kindly portrayal of the manufacturer here, a touch of a leer on a labor organizer's face there — until still more charts show absorption of the message, up to saturation point, by the public brain.

Few leaders of industry undertake major public-relations campaigns without consulting the pollsters. 'UNDERSTAND RIVALRY AND YOU UNDERSTAND AMERICA!' a nationwide 'Americanism' ad of the Petroleum Institute of America proclaims in the magazines. The ad, of course, was sent off to be tested. The result of the test, as reported by the Psychological Corporation, one of the largest U.S. market-research organizations:

'Readability; easy. 5th grade. Like pulp fiction. Potential audience, 86 per cent of U.S. adults.'

The pollsters are at work in every field of mass communication; in radio, television, magazines, the movies, and even books. In the radio and television industries alone there are concentrated the efforts of at least half a dozen major polling organizations which launch statistical inquiries into the people's listening habits and rate competing programs accordingly. In the luxurious advertising offices along Madison Avenue, the pollster's word on what programs the people prefer is law.

Until recently few advertising executives dared stir abroad without a small green booklet known as the *Hooperatings Pocket Piece* about their persons. Over a period of a dozen years, this charmed inventory, issued by C. E. Hooper, Inc., a polling organization, became widely revered as the bible of radio and television. The Hooper rating reduced to an aggregation of digits and decimal points the size of each network program's invisible audience. Its influence was enormous. An acquaintance of mine, having been advised to listen on his radio to a new chamber-music group, once mentioned the program to a network executive he met at a cocktail party. 'I hear it's pretty good,' my friend remarked. The network chief whipped out his handy rating booklet and began riffling the pages. 'Well, fair,' he said with a frown when he found the right entry. 'Just fair.'

In 1950 Hooper, who snooped upon the nation's viewing and listening habits by telephone, sold out part of his business to a rival, A. C. Nielsen, who interviews the people electromagnetically with a device called the Audimeter. Wired to sample radio and television sets in homes throughout the country, the Audimeter automatically records on tape every turn of the dials to which it is connected. Roaming abroad in pre-arranged formation, Nielsen agents enter representative homes, connect their Audimeters to all radio and television sets within reach, and retire to headquarters while the machines record the sample listeners' choice of programs. Having observed its hosts' taste for a sufficient period, the Audimeter ejects two quarters with a tinkle of thanks and the request that the recording tape be mailed to Nielsen GHQ for tabulation.

Some idea of the stakes involved in the poll business may be gleaned from the fact that Nielsen has invested some seven million dollars in his Audimeter system, including gigantic electronic computers. Each of these has three thousand tubes, and is designed to register popular reaction with the speed of light, and neatly to compute its mercantile possibilities by way of twenty thousand multiplications or divisions per second.

Nielsen has explained the need for all his formidable apparatus this way: 'The sponsor, faced with the dire necessity of selling more goods per dollar expended, says: "An increase from eighty to eighty-eight is a gain of ten per cent. And since my program costs one million dollars a year, that's like finding a cool hundred thousand." This "financial viewpoint" — this realization that sound audience-research figures are not dry statistics but may be converted directly into cold, hard dollars — is one of the outstanding trends today.'

In the past, Nielsen's machines and Hooper's telephone calls frequently rendered quite different estimates about what share of the radio or television audience was being captured by which artists. A sponsor who might be impelled to give his radio or television comedian a handsome bonus on the basis of Nielsen ratings might contrarily, on the basis of Hooper's findings, be constrained to fire him. Many advertising executives resolved cantankerous problems of this sort by buying both services — and others too — and displaying to the sponsor whichever chart gave their programs the higher rating.

The deference to ratings in the world of radio and television over the years, has assumed reverential proportions, and the pattern of programs on any network is constantly being juggled around in accordance with the fluctuations of the magic numbers assigned them by polling organizations. Some networks and advertising agencies write audience-rating clauses into artists' contracts. CBS, for example, was reported at one time to have made a contract with the American Tobacco Company under which the network obligated itself to pay a forfeit if the audience rating of the comedian, Jack Benny, fell below the level established for him. For each audience-rating point lost over a specified period of time the network was to be penalized three thousand dollars.

Under such circumstances, the appearance of the rating chart is naturally a matter of grave significance around the agencies and networks. Vice-presidents wade up and down through the thick carpets, quoting the latest ratings in the same rapid-fire fashion as downtown Wall Street stockbrokers toss off the latest curb opening prices. A slight decline of the program's rating, and a troupe of unfortunate artists may be expelled from the studios. A steady lag, and an advertising account worth millions of dollars may be transferred to another agency. The effects of the rating are felt down through the ranks, to the lowliest gag writer.

Few producers of programs dare allow the ratings of their shows to drop without resorting to strenuous counter-action. 'If you find your rating wavering,' one program director remarked, 'you can always throw in a guest star. That costs you

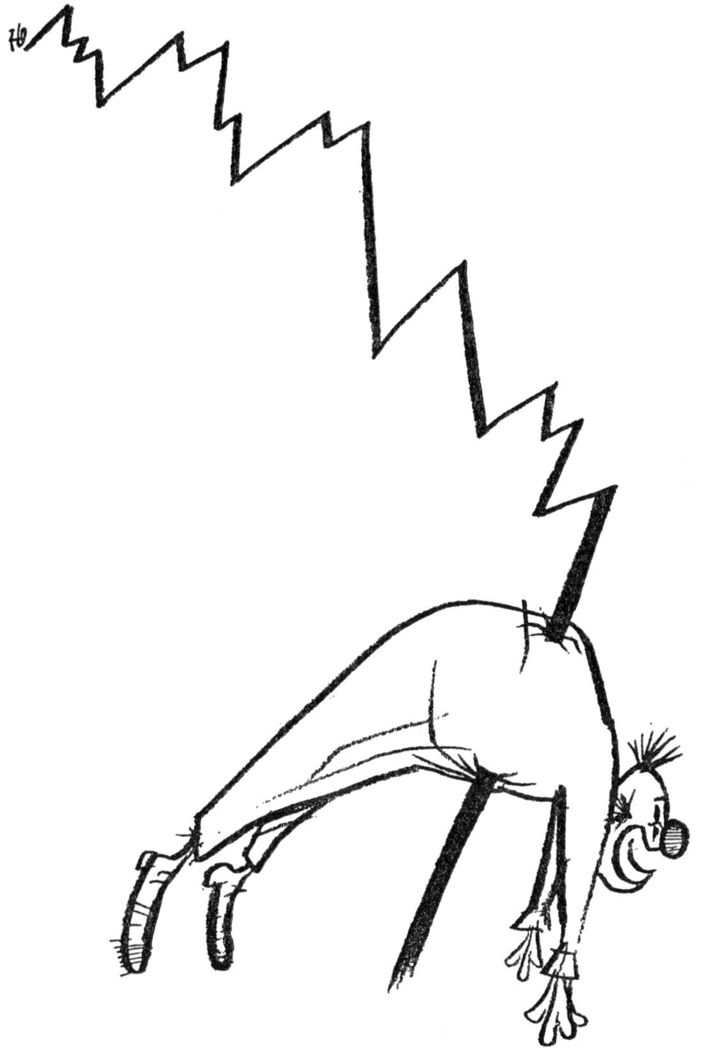

up to ten thousand dollars, but it usually jacks your rating up five points. Two grand a point. Cheap at the price.'

Some radio artists do not take kindly to the rating system. Fred Allen, whose rating once dipped violently under the competing influence of an adjacent give-away show, sullenly remarked that the radio pollsters 'could count the bottom of a bird cage and tell you how many grains of sand there are in the Sahara desert.' He went on to imply that ratings were not the best test of an actor's artistic worth. The remark was of course coolly received within the top echelons of the radio business.

Not content with the independent rating services they subscribe to, most of the radio and television networks maintain their own bureaus, and a remarkable variety of snooping machines, to pre-test audience reactions to their programs.

CBS, for example, uses the Lazarsfeld-Stanton Program Analyzer, a mass of wires, pointers, and capillary pens familiarly known to CBS people in its two versions as 'Little Annie' and 'Big Annie.' Little Annie pre-tests the reactions of groups of ten to fifteen people; Big Annie takes on seventy-five to one hundred.

A group delivering itself into the arms of Little Annie sits cozily around a table and registers reactions to a program by pushing colored buttons, green for approval and red for disapproval. The buttons are wired into a near-by studio where each spasm of like or dislike is recorded on moving tapes by capillary pens.

Nearly a thousand CBS shows have been pre-tested in this way, and a number of artists have been placed beyond the pale as a result. One program stuffed into the maw of Little Annie was a quiz show. CBS had already determined a splendid formula of what it called 'listener gratifications' for this kind of program: 'Self testing, fifty-five per cent; humor, forty-five per cent; prizes, forty-two per cent; information, thirty per cent; human interest, fourteen per cent; and contest, ten per cent.'

To CBS the quiz program being pre-tested fell short of this ideal recipe. 'The high spots of the graph coincided with the quiz, the low spots with the quizmaster's gags,' a CBS official said in discussing the outcome. 'That showed us that people didn't want a quizmaster turned comedian. We fired the quizmaster.'

Little Annie's guests are supposed to represent a cross section of the population. Actually most of them are drawn from studio audiences, or invited in off the streets. When I dropped in at CBS's psychological laboratories one day to observe Little Annie at work, the audience consisted of ten people, most of them middle-aged and quite well dressed. These, it was explained to me, were only part of the total group to be tested — some seventy-five people in all. The program to be audience-tested was a television drama.

The lights were lowered, a sound film of the show was thrown on to a screen, and the CBS psychologist in charge of the seance retired to the next room to observe the reactions of Little Annie. I went along with him. As the show progressed, needles on the machine began to click, furiously registering approval here, disapproval there.

'Number Four doesn't like the narrator,' said the executive, scribbling hurriedly. 'Number Eight's wavering.' The needles clicked away. 'Number Seven likes the heroine,' said the executive. 'But watch Number Four! See that needle? Number Four just can't stand the narrator.'

Ten more minutes and Little Annie had registered by capillary pen an emphatic line of hatred for the narrator by Number Four. After the program ended the members of the audience were given cigarettes ('to put them at ease') and invited to indulge in what a CBS booklet calls 'oral articulation.' This consisted of answering such questions as: 'Number Three, how did you like the show? Did you think it was okay?' Most of the people thought that it wasn't.

Just as the people were about to be thanked and sent on their ways (the remaining cigarettes were already locked up in a drawer), the CBS psychologist asked, 'How did you like the narrator, Number Four?' Number Four turned out to be a middle-aged lady with a high-pitched voice and a large hat. 'Oh,' said Number Four, 'I liked him fine.' She had evidently been pressing the wrong button, thus by proxy bringing down on the narrator the curse of millions. I don't know what happened to the narrator, but the damning evidence lay entrenched somewhere in Little Annie's intricate intestines.

Aside from the over-all reaction testing machines, there are a number of specialty devices, ranging all the way from the Ernest Walker Gag Meter, for rating the effectiveness of comedians' jokes, to the Psycho-Galvanometer, rating the effectiveness of commercials. The Gag Meter supplies a mathematically expressed index to the amount of laughter evoked by a witticism. The Psycho-Galvanometer enables advertisers to judge the effectiveness of their commercials by actually measuring the degree to which they make their listeners sweat.

A subject undergoing the Psycho-Galvanometer test appears, at first sight, to have been prepared for the electric chair. Attached to his forearm and palm are electrodes with wires running to a maze of tapes and needles. The commercial is then shouted at him over powerful loud-speakers, and the listener sweats in degrees theoretically related to his emotional responses to what he hears. The sweat alters the electrical resistance of his skin, which perks up the Psycho-Galvanometer, and the Psycho-Galvanometer, in turn, records its reactions on moving tape. The more perspiration, the more effective the commercial. This is called the 'arousal method.' Singing commercials are said to cause very high arousals. A remarkable instance of the value of the arousal test has been reported by the

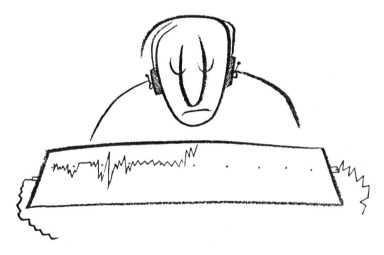

advertising firm of Gilliland, Ranseen, Wesley, and Ragan. One woman, during lengthy questioning, had expressed a low opinion of Gene Autry, a horseman heavily subsidized by, among other corporations, the William Wrigley, Jr., Company. She was then wired up to the Psycho-Galvanometer and exposed to a recorded Autry program. The lady was said to have perspired profusely, and finally to have cried: 'Gene Autry can sell me anything!'

'Had this woman been on a panel of any research study

which did not use an electronic recorder of emotional response,' the agency reported, 'she would have been reported a non-listener to Autry.'

The big advertising agency of Ruthrauff and Ryan has been probing even deeper than the Psycho-Galvanometer into the American mind. For more than a year the agency has been resorting to the services of a prominent hypnotist. The job of this man has been to put selected consumers into hypnotic sleep and keenly to question them about their likes, their dislikes, their motivations, and, of course, their reactions to Ruthrauff and Ryan advertising. Even in the unconscious there is no refuge. Millions are at stake.

Television, as might be expected, gets its full quota of attention from the pollsters, and one of the corporate arms of the Gallup organization, Audience Research Institute, Inc., has done a good deal of research in that field. Some time ago, I was fortunate enough to observe the results of an A.R.I. experiment. A Gallup official brought out a large sheet of paper on which a stretch of programs had been compressed into an 'attitude graph,' and he began tracing the progress of part of an evening of television.

First came a newsreel, which showed as a series of dips and peaks varying from 'good,' for a picture of a gas explosion, to 'neutral,' for a singing commercial. A movie featuring Rudy Vallee and a number of hunting dogs followed. Upon the appearance of the hounds, the graph soared; on the presentation of Mr. Vallee, it sank.

The program ended with a movie short of the American flag, while the accompanying orchestra played *The Star Spangled Banner*. The reaction of Gallup's typical Americans to the appearance of their country's flag varied from 'neutral' to 'good' — a clear case for Senator McCarthy.

Gallup's Audience Research Institute has also done work in the motion-picture field. As other market researchers rate brand preferences in canned soups, so the Institute rates preferences in canned daydreams. It does not pre-test only finished films. It submits them to the public at any or every stage of their development, from little more than a glazed look in a producer's eye to a boiler-plate ad for the finished movie. Roughly, the process, as I gathered it from the Gallup people some time ago, works as follows:

A producer is given an idea for a movie. He turns it over to A.R.I., whose Ph.D's summarize it in sixty words on 'subject-matter test' cards. These are submitted for approval or disapproval to a cross section of the people, and the idea is rated accordingly. On the basis of the subject-matter rating, according to A.R.I., producers can then decide 'whether to purchase the property, or where to assign the idea.'

Titles are tested in the same way. Then comes the problem of the stars for the movie, and for this Gallup's men run an 'audit of marquee values.' In one case, for example, a producer couldn't make up his mind whether to co-star Dana Andrews with June Allyson or Betty Grable.

'In the first cast,' said a Gallup official, 'we found that Dana Andrews came up with a marquee rating of twenty-nine for men and forty-one for women. Total rating of thirty-five. Allyson's total rating was thirty-four. In the second cast, Grable had an actually lower total rating than Allyson — only thirty-three. But they chose Grable. Why? Our sex breakdown showed Grable rated thirty-six with men, which was higher than Allyson's man rating. The Grable-Andrews combination showed a better balance of appeal between the sexes.'

Before the film is released, it undergoes an A.R.I. 'audience profile test' on a gadget called the Hopkins Televoter. A small theater is filled with three hundred or more people scientifically selected by Gallup's agents. As the film is shown, the people record their reactions by twisting individual dials marked from 'poor' to 'good.' Every dialed reaction is reported backstage by the Hopkins Televoter in the form of a composite graph. The level of the graph dictates additional cutting or perhaps additional shooting. In the case of the movie *Gilda*, for example, the Televoter indicated that people weren't sure at one point of the film whether a certain character was alive or not. As a result, a sea-rescue scene was inserted, and an A.R.I. official told me, 'the graph picked up beautifully and leveled right off.'

The *Gilda* graph had previously been displayed to me by another Gallup man. It was yards long. As it unrolled before my eyes I noticed that at about the halfway mark the graph suddenly dipped violently into the category of 'poor.' I asked the reason. The Gallup man looked puzzled. 'I don't recall, exactly,' he murmured, 'but it certainly looks bad. I'll look it up.' He went to a file cabinet, shuffled through some papers, then came back. 'I see now what the problem was,' he reported. 'The film was burning in the projector gate.'

In computing their sample, A.R.I. statisticians carefully subtract from the population the blind or deaf (400,000), institutionalized criminals, the insane, and sick (1,000,000), the aged and infirm (4,000,000), and children under twelve (29,400,000). Mathematically, that should leave approximately 112 million Americans, but the movie audience sampled by Gallup actually amounts to only sixty-five million people, leav-

ing a residue of forty-seven million people somehow disfranchised.

The reason for this is that Gallup questions only those who say they have been to a movie in the last three weeks (a universe of 65,000,000). Movie admissions bought by people under thirty amount to 61 per cent of the total — at thirty the moviegoer, like the combat pilot, is considered to be pretty well done for. Since these statistics govern Gallup's choice, his universe is peopled primarily by the young. The more mature in years, and those millions who find enough fault with the movies not to see them regularly, apparently are ignored as statistical dross.

When questioned about the refinements of this process, which might be comparable to a political election in which only those who like the Administration may vote, A.R.I. officials point out that Gallup has constantly urged the movie industry to widen its audience. I asked an A.R.I. official why Gallup didn't widen *his* audience. 'Frankly, it's too expensive,' he replied.

No peep into artistic research would be complete without a glance at the operations of a former Gallup executive named Albert E. Sindlinger. Shortly after Sindlinger left the Gallup organization several years ago, he moved in on Broadway, with the backing of Walter E. Heller, the chief of a huge Chicago investment syndicate. Heller wished to invest money in Broadway plays, and Sindlinger undertook to tell him, by means of graphs showing audience reactions to recorded synopses of potential plays, which plays were likely to gross the most. 'We pre-tested eighteen plays,' Sindlinger told me with satisfaction, 'and we rejected nine as bad investments. Of the other nine, eight were hits and one didn't go well but won a critics' award.'

Having put Broadway on a graph, Sindlinger then repaired to his farm in Hopewell, New Jersey, to devise a suitable statistical formula for turning book manuscripts into best sellers. In this large endeavor he had the help of an electro-mechanical editor of his own contrivance, which went under the name of Teldox. To Teldox a manuscript into fame, Sindlinger would first pass it to his apprentices, who boiled it, like an old fowl, down to its bones. In skeletal form, the story was then narrated by a professional announcer and transcribed onto an hour-long recording. Sindlinger would then bring in a sample audience and play the recorded synopsis to it. As the book's message soaked in, the audience, which had been fed a light snack, recorded its reactions, ranging from 'superior' to 'bad,' on Teldox switches. The inevitable reaction graph was made up, and then the author, or Sindlinger's laboratory assistants, would begin the task of reshaping the book. Sindlinger

116

never accepted a fixed fee for his Teldox literary services, but contented himself instead with a percentage of the author's total royalties, ranging from 10 to 50 per cent.

As an example of the literary miracles worked by Teldox, Sindlinger has cited the case of Sterling North, who, in 1943, wrote a children's book called *Midnight and Jeremiah*, which he later rewrote as *So Dear To My Heart*. North decided to submit the later manuscript to Teldox — or, as he put it in his book-review columns, to 'the collective wisdom of the American people.' Sindlinger has it that North rewrote the end of the book as indicated by Teldox. The resulting work sold extremely well and was later made into a highly successful movie — a thoroughly pre-tested movie, of course. 'I'm just trying to stimulate creative writing,' Sindlinger told me.

The Smoke-filled Barn

The legend of Aaron, who fashioned a golden calf and commanded the people to fall down and worship it, is generally speaking an instructive one. The Children of Israel obeyed him, but not for long, and soon he was out of business. History has known many golden calves, and many Aarons. But I doubt whether it has known the likes of the Borden Company, one of our great American corporations. The Borden Company might be said to have taken up where Aaron left off and where he failed, to have succeeded. It has raised into the arena of public idolatry not a calf, it is true, but a cow: Elsie the Cow. Perhaps no more fitting tribute to the golden influence of this American totem exists than the fact that the Borden Company, its owner, is grossing more than $500 million each year through the sale of dairy products, such as Borden's Milk, Borden's Eagle Brand Sweetened Condensed Milk, Borden's Ice Cream, and Borden's Fine Cheeses. Elsie the Cow is the advertising symbol of this corporate kingdom, its power and glory. The mayors of fourteen California cities once prostrated themselves before a live, lowing, representation of Elsie when she emerged from a plane at the San Francisco airport. This deferential gesture, which involved a proffering to Elsie the Cow of the keys to their respective cities, would probably be regarded as a triumph of mercantilism in less fully industrialized countries, but to Borden's it was more or less routine. To date, Elsie the Cow has received the keys to seventy-four cities, and to five states, and other keys are still being presented. The educators are not far behind the alderman; the cow has been made the recipient of honorary degrees by several institutions of higher learning.

To determine the extent of the animal's popularity, Borden's intermittently has had several public-opinion polls made on the subject of Elsie. In 1945, her picture was identified correctly by 58 per cent of people interrogated about her. This figure perhaps becomes more meaningful when compared with the recognition rating of other public figures, such as Albert Einstein (48 per cent), James F. Byrnes, then Secretary of State (44 per cent), and Van Johnson, the movie star (43 per cent). A later survey, made just before the presidential elections in 1948, showed the cow as having a recognition rating of 88 per cent, a figure exceeded only by President Truman's 93 per cent. More people recognized Elsie than Thomas E. Dewey, who was generally thought a sure bet to win the election, or Dwight D. Eisenhower, whose recognition factor came to only 83 per cent, or 5 per cent lower than Elsie's. Another poll showed Elsie's rating to be 23.3 per cent higher than that of Fred Vinson, the late Chief Justice of the Supreme Court — a natural enough result, since the decisions and dissents of Elsie the Cow generally get considerably more space in American newspapers and magazines than did those of the Chief Justice. Cartoon advertisements bearing the beast's likeness are regularly spread over entire pages of national magazines whose combined circulation totals more than 30 million.

Elsie the Cow, as an advertising cartoon figure, was conceived by the Borden people in 1936 owing to a lamentable measure of public misunderstanding on the subject of giant milk companies. 'In many markets the fluid milk distributor . . . is pictured as a gouger, a bandit, and an octopus, in spite of the fact that he is extremely lucky if he can make as much as a fraction of a cent on a quart of milk, and frequently sells at a loss,' Stuart Peabody, the director of advertising for the Borden Company sadly wrote in the magazine *Advertising & Selling*, in describing this sentiment. 'We reasoned that our advertising approach should be a human one, and, most of all, friendly,' he went on to add, more cheerfully. The most immediate result of this reasoning was the experimental insertion by the Borden Company, in 1936, of a number of advertisements in medical journals showing, in caricature, a number of cows chatting among themselves about Borden's. The advertisements were successful enough to bring in a number of requests from physicians for copies of them suitable to be framed and put on walls of their waiting rooms. The series of advertisements was continued in medical journals until 1938, when the Borden Farm Products Division, the company's fluid milk unit in New York, began advertising in local newspapers with similar cartoons. The name Elsie did not appear in them, however — it was first used later, by a radio announcer who happened to include it in one of his commercials for the Borden Company. By 1939 Borden's took to the name, and concept, and began promoting the cartoon character of Elsie, the Borden Cow, in national magazine advertisements. The character became so popular that at the Borden exhibit at the New York World's

Fair, in 1939, attendants were constantly asked by visitors, 'Where's Elsie?'

Up to that time the Borden people, who had 150 cows on exhibition at the Fair, hadn't given any thought to the representation of Elsie in anything but advertising cartoons, but now, in view of the obvious public desire to see an Elsie in the flesh, they chose a Jersey named 'You'll Do, Lobelia,' draped her in a green blanket embroidered with the name 'Elsie,' and put her on display by herself. The promotion went into high gear; by the spring of 1940, Borden publicity men were distributing to Fair visitors free pamphlets describing the cow's schedule thus:

This summer, Elsie will live in a glass house! Literally. The most pampered bucolic belle of the times will dwell, indeed, in a glass-fronted, spacious, lavishly appointed boudoir — Elsie actually will reside in bed, standing among the posts of a canopied bed of exaggerated proportions. As a preventative of nostalgia, the wallpaper will portray pastoral scenes. Elsie will have, of course, her dressing table — with mirror, brushes, cosmetics incident of a distinguished beauty's vanity assembly . . .

From time to time, between appearances at the Fair, the cow was shuttled around to various affairs, such as a reception at the Roosevelt Hotel, in New York, at which Elsie was installed in a private dining room, and a Bovine Ball held by a National Guard Regiment, at which the cow was the guest of honor. She rode the elevators of high-class hotels across the country. In Hollywood, she played with Kay Francis in a film called *Little Men*. During her absences from the World's Fair, another cow was slyly substituted in Flushing Meadow for

124

Elsie, but a considerable part of the visiting public, learning from the press of Elsie's appearances elsewhere, apparently considered the substitution a shallow deceit. Borden's public-relations men quickly reacted to this temporary setback by installing a bull, Elmer, in its World's Fair exhibit and spreading the idea that he was Elsie's husband and was keeping house for Elsie in her absence. The fiction appeared acceptable to many, and later, despite the fact that the bull in question was of such sluggish disposition that he ignored altogether twenty other cows on display with him at the Fair, Borden's publicity department showed no hesitation in proclaiming him the father when Elsie bore a calf, which they christened Beulah.

The publicity attending this affair was, naturally, enormous. Film stars, or their press agents, sent appropriate presents, and congratulations poured in by wire and mail from the general public. An astrologer went to the trouble of predicting Elsie's future on the basis of the configuration of star phenomena on her day of birth. He predicted, among other things, that she would die of old age. Actually, the cow came to an untimely end while traveling by truck from a farm in New Jersey to a lunch at Sardi's. The truck was involved in a collision, and You'll Do, Lobelia was mortally injured. This was in May, 1941, just before the German invasion of Russia. Many people appeared saddened at the news of the cow's death. So was Borden's. Elsie had already been scheduled to put in appearances at trade-association meetings and state fairs, and her demise affected not only many such commitments but the very foundations of Borden's campaign against the ever-insidious anti-Big Milk sentiment. 'Everybody in the company was deeply grieved,' its advertising director later wrote in an obituary for the milk trade. 'They sincerely loved the cow. Those of us concerned with promotion were prostrated. The publicity of the cow's death topped anything she had had before. Clippings, wires, letters of condolence, flowers, came in from all parts of the country. The whole promotion seemed about to collapse.'

The funeral meats were scarcely cold, however, before Borden's bounced back into action. The company selected not another cow but three cows, and named them all Elsie. The legend lives on, the triple identity, even among Borden's publicity men, being considered for general purposes as one organism. Only one cow goes on tour, for exhibition at various fairs, at a time. By 1953, something like 30 million people were estimated to have viewed one or the other of the cows traveling under the Elsie name.

The choice of a new live Elsie, which has to be made from time to time, is a difficult one involving the best brains from Borden's public-relations staff. The beast must be admired not only by the general public but by farmers. And it must, of course, be photogenic, as well as an outstanding specimen of the breed. 'The first cow we had on display at the World's Fair looked like an immigrant,' a Borden man once told me. 'It was a big Ayrshire. But this Jersey, You'll Do, Lobelia, had the best face you ever saw — a cute-dish puss. I was looking over another candidate the other day. She was type-y, mind, a good Jersey, but she wouldn't appeal to city people, I turned her down.'

In drawings, as distinct from on the hoof, Elsie is endowed with almost human characteristics, all of which are incorporated with great care and precision. Borden artists and copywriters who compose advertisements about her are strictly governed by a set of moral and artistic rules detailed in a com-

pany directive. The directive specifies, for example, that what it refers to, somewhat coyly, as 'Elsie's milk department' may be shown *only* when she is in the natural position of a real cow, on all fours. 'Whenever shown standing or in any other "human" position,' the directive says, 'the udder must be concealed by a leg or some device such as an apron.' Elsie may never be drawn in profile, for some reason that the directive does not explain. Part of her cloven hooves may be used as a thumb, but must never be shaped like one. Her eyes must never be drawn with too much of a slant, for this imparts to the cow's face a prurient and wolf-like leer. The beast may be attractive, but not sensual. The eyes must never be drawn too far back. This is likely to give Elsie a mean look, which, as can be seen from the Borden commandments reported in ensuing paragraphs, is contrary to the animal's whole attitude toward life. On the other hand, if the eyes are drawn too far forward, Elsie assumes a calf-like look. This, too, is out. A calf does not provide milk. The animal must be mature and graceful too. Elsie does not clomp around the house. The Borden directive decrees that the cow shall have 'graceful, feminine hands and arms,' that her ankles shall be 'slim,' her feet 'smallish,' and the snout short and tapering. A slight deviation in following this last instruction can result in Elsie's taking on the characteristics of a sow.

A similar set of instructions are in force to govern the appearance of Elmer, her mate, who, in Borden advertising dramas, acts as a sort of foil for Elsie's epigrams, as well as Beulah, the female offspring, and Beauregard, later-added male calf of the family.

The personality of Elsie the cow-human is also very carefully kept in check. Borden's advertising department has issued a confidential bulletin on this for the guidance of its various units. Among other things, the bulletin lays down these points:

. . . We felt that unless we made up our minds as to just what sort of a character she was she might get out of control . . . We spent many hours with our creative people and with the [advertising] agency determining what manner of person Elsie was . . .

Elsie is one of the strongest personalities of public life . . . She combines the role of mother and career woman. In the latter respect she is not necessarily the Helen Hokinson type of clubwoman or the small-town housewife . . . While her home-and-mother role is her first love, she is a delightful kind of gadabout, frequently on the move.

Elsie never evidences a touch of phony sophistication . . . is an exponent of the cracker-barrel school of simple, human philosophy. She is 'dumb' only in one respect. She is single-track-minded . . . about Borden . . .

She is at all times too capable to be reduced to the feminine device of tears . . . She is playful and likes her little joke, but her jokes are more apologetic puns than flip wisecracks . . . She is never slangy, never common or vulgar. Her only remarks which approach slang are those with a certain prim, Victorian feeling . . .

It was presumably in deference to Victorianism that Borden's public-relations men declined, on the occasion of Elsie's visit to the Dallas Fair, an offer by Gypsy Rose Lee for a publicity tieup. The dignity of the cow's stature in American life could not permit the association. As one Borden executive remarked later, 'the damn cow's on a par with Mother Goose or even George Washington.'

'Say,' he added thoughtfully, after a short pause, 'that's an idea. George Washington. I'll see how he compares in the next recognition poll.'

The

Amphibious

PEN

When the ball-point pen, which once sold for as much as nineteen dollars and ninety-eight cents and which can now be bought at Woolworth's for a quarter — a markdown of approximately 99 per cent — burst upon the country two months after the end of the Second World War, the writing public was in a highly receptive mood. At nine-thirty on the morning of 29 October 1945, when Gimbel's ('Good old Gimbel's, the plain store for plain people') first placed on sale 'the miraculous pen that will revolutionize writing,' five thousand people were waiting to swarm through the doors, and fifty extra policemen were hastily dispatched to restrain the throng. Inside the store, where ball-point pens lay heaped in gleaming piles on the counters of two aisles running almost the entire length of the Thirty-second Street side, buying quickly reached the proportions of a stampede. In an attempt to break up the jam, Gimbel's hurriedly set up emergency counters, and during the day, as fresh supplies of pens were rushed to the city by plane, placed them on sale in other departments. 'We took over Umbrellas, we knocked out Clocks, and we went into Silver,' a Gimbel's man told me in recalling the event. 'There were ball-point pens all over the place.' The pens sold for twelve dollars and fifty cents apiece, and some people bought dozens. They were guaranteed to write for two years without refilling, to write without leaking not only on the ground but under water and at stratospheric altitudes, and to make a clear impression on from six to eight carbons. By the end of the day, Gimbel's had sold ten thousand ball-point pens — a hundred and twenty-five thousand dollars' worth at retail, representing just about a third of the store's average total daily sales volume at that time. Within a few days, the ball-point-pen fever began to take hold elsewhere. In Miami, proprietors of fruit stands sold ball-point pens to customers who stopped by for a drink of orange juice. Fly-by-night stores opened up in San Francisco to sell nothing but ball-point pens. Dressmakers sold them. They appeared in gas stations, jewelry stores, barbershops, men's-furnishings stores, and highway hot-dog stands. And everywhere they were swept away as fast as they came in. It was, indeed, a pen manufacturer's dream — for all but those who had pioneered in the development of the ball-point pen, and they were beside themselves with chagrin. Someone had stolen their thunder.

Actually, there was nothing particularly new about the principles of the ball-point pen. During the war, American fliers who had occasion to stop off in Argentina found ball-point pens in the shops there and brought back numbers of them to pass around as novelties among their friends. These pens were the handiwork of Laszlo Jozsef Biro, a Hungarian who had been, at one time or another, a medical student, a painter, a sculptor, a hypnotist, a journalist, and a proofreader. Biro, who felt the need of a ball-point pen after splaying innumberable fountain-pen points on newspaper proofs, made one in Paris and took out a patent on it there in 1939. Shortly afterward, he moved to Buenos Aires, and, in 1943, he interested an English financier named Henry G. Martin, who had also moved to Buenos Aires, in backing the manufacture of the pen on a modest scale. For this purpose, a company known as Eterpen S.A. was set up, with Martin at its head. The Biro pen differed from conventional fountain pens in three important respects. First, instead of a nib it had a miniature socket which held a ball bearing one millimeter in diameter; second, instead of using ordinary ink it contained a gelatinous dye with an oil base that, rolled onto a writing surface by the ball bearing which it at the same time lubricated, dried almost instantly; and, third, it held enough of this unconventional ink to perform for several months without refilling. The special nature of the ink also made it possible for the pen to be used at high altitudes without the risk of leakage that ordinary fountain pens, because of the effect a change in atmospheric pressure has on liquid, have always been subject to. This particular advantage appealed to the Royal Air Force, whose bomber crews had been constantly plagued by leaky fountain pens. Before long, Martin and Biro farmed out the British rights to a British aircraft company. In the closing months of the war, the United States Air Force also became interested in the ball-point idea and sent some of the pens around to various American manufacturers, with word that it might be interested in buying ten thousand or so of them. At this, the three big pen-manufacturing concerns in this country — Parker, Sheaffer, and Eversharp — began looking into the matter of patent rights and discovered that the United States rights had already been acquired by Eberhard Faber, the pencil-manufacturing firm, which had originally planned to manufacture the pen but had run into difficulties. The big companies, and several smaller ones, immediately started dickering with Eberhard Faber for a share in the rights. Martin L. Straus, then president of Eversharp, won out, and in the spring of 1945 two agreements were signed involving Eversharp, Eberhard Faber, and Eterpen. The terms of these were extremely complicated, but in essence Eversharp and Eberhard Faber committed themselves to pay Eterpen a royalty of 5¼ per cent on the American sales of the pen; Eversharp and Eberhard Faber bought outright from Eterpen, for a total of half a million dollars, the rights to the pen in the Caribbean and Philippine areas; and Eberhard Faber agreed to share its American rights with Eversharp, while Eversharp undertook to manufacture certain ball-point-pen parts not only for itself but for the pencil company, if and when it wanted any. Straus, who during the war years had been promoting, among other items, a solid-gold pen and pencil set priced at a hundred and twenty-five dollars (he sold fifty thousand of them in two years), was delighted with his acquisition and foresaw large profits once certain defects in it had been ironed out. 'The original Biro model was a leaker,' he said later. 'It skipped, it stuck, it wrote a very fine line, and under certain climatic conditions it didn't write at all. But it was very revolutionary.'

Straus turned the pen over to his engineers, instructing them to redesign it with an eye to mass production, and then instituted an advertising campaign to prepare the public for his new 'miracle pen,' as he described it in one brochure. The campaign was a success. Interest in the pen quickly became widespread. The advertising, which cost Straus a considerable amount of money, was particularly pleasing to Gimbel's, because Gimbel's was just about to bring out its 'new atomic-era miraculous fountain pen you've heard about, read about, waited for.' As it happened, this pen was not the Eversharp pen, for Eversharp's engineers were still busy at their drawing boards, but one produced by Milton Reynolds, a man who had had no previous experience in the pen business. The coup, which had been very carefully planned, put Reynolds' company in the 70-per cent tax bracket within a week.

Reynolds, a short, bespectacled, gregarious, globular man with an Elkish buoyancy, a vast gift for persuasion, and a restless instinct for selling things, had first seen the Biro pen in June, 1945, four months before the Gimbel coup. He saw it in a Buenos Aires store during a business tour he was making of South America, and he immediately decided that it was a winner. Although he knew nothing about pens, he knew a good deal about the retail market back home. As president of the Printasign Corporation of America, a Chicago firm that was making, and still makes, a kind of oversize typewriter for turning out display cards for stores, he was in touch with the managers of practically all the department stores in the United States, and he was fully aware that they, facing what might well be their first postwar Christmas season, were harassed by shortages and desperate for novelty gifts that could be quickly manufactured with such materials as were at hand. He had had experience along similar lines in 1944, when, acquiring a batch of silver cigarette lighters in Mexico, he flew them to lighterless American department stores just in time for the peak of the Christmas trade. Reynolds cleaned up a quarter of a million dollars on lighters and then went out of the lighter business. He had long before mastered the art of plunging into a quick deal.

As for the art of pulling out of it at the right moment, his sensitivity had been sharpened over the years by the loss of three fortunes.

Reynolds was born in Albert Lea, Minnesota, in 1892, the son of a threshing-machine salesman. Upon flunking his first semester of high school, he set out for Chicago with the idea of making a million dollars, which he had succeeded in doing by the time he was twenty-six, on an initial outlay of twenty-five dollars, by organizing and running a string of tire shops specializing in manufacturers' seconds. By the time he was thirty, he had lost his million in the stock market. In 1925, he borrowed some money and headed for the Florida land-boom country, and again became rich, this time as one of the first builders of prefabricated houses, buying parts in New Orleans and shipping them by caravans of barges to their destination. A year later, his second fortune disappeared, along with one of his caravans, its crew, and a cargo of unassembled houses, off the Florida coast during a hurricane. The storm blew Reynolds back to Chicago, where he talked himself into a job as president of a company that sold quotation boards to stockbrokerage houses. He was wealthy again by 1929, when the stock market crash did him in.

Cleaned out for the third time, Reynolds started prowling the Loop district of Chicago in search of new money-making ideas. On the third day, peering through the window of a small, dusty printing shop, he saw a crude model of the Printasign. Investigation revealed that the proprietor of the shop owned the rights to the machine, and Reynolds talked him into selling them to him on credit. Reynolds made a good thing out of Printasigns and gradually expanded his market as far as South America, but he remained constantly on the alert for what he called 'the big idea.' That was what he sensed he had found when he came across the Biro pen in Buenos Aires, and he hunted up its inventor. Biro told him affably that the American rights to the pen had already been picked up. This information was far from disheartening to Reynolds, for he had learned enough in the business world to be skeptical of the protection afforded by patents. Pleasantly taking his leave of Biro, he flew home with several of the new pens. En route, he wired an engineer he knew to meet him at the Chicago airport. 'I wasn't afraid of whatever patents Eterpen might have,' Reynolds says. 'And something told me I was carrying a million dollars in my breast pocket.' As soon as he arrived in Chicago, Reynolds, together with the engineer, headed for the nearest patent library. There Reynolds' casual attitude toward Eterpen's patent rights shortly proved to be, at least in part, well founded. The principle of a pen with a ball point, Reynolds discovered, was comparatively ancient history in this country; a man named John Loud had patented it in 1888, and seventeen years later it had entered the public domain without ever having been exploited. One point covered by the Biro patent, however, was not so easily ignored. This was the matter of feeding the ink evenly onto the ball bearing. Biro had at first tried to do it by regulating the pressure of the ink with a screw at the top of the pen, a method that had previously been patented in Prague by two Czechoslovakians, Paul V. Eisner and Wenzel Klimes. (Eisner and Klimes had, in fact, marketed a ball-point pen in Europe for a few years, though with little success; they had also sought to sell the idea of the pen to American manufacturers, with no success at all.) Biro found the pressure-feed system cumbersome and went on to develop a feeder mechanism based on the principle of capillary attraction, and it was this that was used in the pens Reynolds had picked up in Buenos Aires.

After much thought, and a number of long and feverish days in a tumble-down machine shop, during which Reynolds and his engineer designed one ball-point pen after another, they devised a way of feeding the ink to the ball bearing by the simple and unpatentable law of gravity. Then came V-J Day. Reynolds cut his hours of sleep to three. 'I knew the pen had to be selling by Christmas of 1945 to be a success,' he says. 'The timing had to be just right. The public wanted a postwar wonder and wanted it then. If the ball-point pen had hit the market one year later, I don't think it would have sold worth a damn.'

Reynolds was putting the finishing touches on his gravity-fed pen when he chanced, late one rainy evening, to be sitting in a bar-and-grill scribbling endlessly with it on a damp newspaper. Gradually, he became conscious that, soggy though the newspaper was, the lines of his scribbling stood out clearly. This struck him as peculiar and, by way of experimenting, he spilled a few drops of water on the table top and tried again, with the same result. Returning to his shop, he put a piece of paper on the bottom of a basin of water and drew a line on it with the pen. Again the line was unblurred. That gave Reynolds precisely the sort of promotional idea he wanted, and led to his coining of the memorable phrase 'It writes under water.' 'The object was to make people tell each other what a ridiculous thing it was to boast about,' he told me. 'While they were telling each other that, they were telling each other about the pen. The publicity was worth millions.'

Shortly after V-J Day, Reynolds sent an emissary with a handmade specimen of his pen to the Office of Price Administration to have that agency set the retail price ceiling then required on new products. 'All the other *shnooks* in the pen business thought you just had to write a letter to O.P.A. to get a decent ceiling,' a Reynolds man has since said. 'Milt is a wonderful opportunist, and of course he wanted to make a buck. The best he thought he could possibly get was a ten-dollar ceiling, but he had the guts to talk them up to twelve-fifty. After all, we had a barrel and a ball, and we could even make it write a little.' In the early stages of production, the pen cost Reynolds about eighty cents to make. (Within three years, thanks to improved methods and cheaper materials, it cost about eight cents.)

Reynolds took his sample pen to Gimbel's and came away with an order for twenty-five hundred. Eversharp got wind of the deal and, according to Reynolds, one evening, in the Stork Club, Straus strolled over to Frederic A. Gimbel, then executive head of the store, and told him he might have a basis for a patent-infringement suit against Gimbel's if it put Reynolds' pen on sale. A few years later, neither Straus nor Gimbel could recall such a meeting, but Reynolds was sure enough that it took place to call it 'the first real break I had.' 'Eversharp couldn't successfully sue me for using a gravity feed, and they knew it,' he says with satisfaction. 'Gimbel's turned around and raised my order to fifty thousand pens. That was a total, at the retail price, of six hundred and twenty-five thousand dollars.'

Having but one pen on hand and no factory in which to work on filling this considerable order, Reynolds engaged a Chicago manufacturer of machine parts, Titus Haffa, to turn out the component parts of his pen, and engaged three hundred people, among them his wife and daughter, to assemble them in a corner of Haffa's plant. The pens were made entirely of war-surplus aluminum, except for the tip, which was made of brass, and the ball bearing, which was made of stainless steel. The barrel was shaped by precision machines normally used in the making of watch movements. The ball bearing was inserted by hand into the tip, which was then mechanically crimped around it to form a socket with a theoretical clearance between the two of one ten-thousandth of an inch. Next, ball and socket were attached to the barrel, and, finally, the special dye was forced into the pen through the microscopic space between ball and socket. Reynolds began mass production of the pen on October sixth, twenty-three days before the Gimbel stampede. His output that first day was seventy ball-point pens.

The day after the first pens were sold at Gimbel's, Reynolds received more orders than it seemed possible to him he could ever fill. 'It was unbelievable,' he said later. 'We had only two phones in the Haffa factory, and some people who tried to call us right after the sale opened had to wait five days to get a clear signal. In the Printasign office, a few blocks away, which we used for clerical work, mail orders were piling up by the bagful, and the phones there were completely jammed, too. The only way we could transact business between the two offices was to send a man out from Printasign to a saloon on the corner every hour and have him call a man from Haffa's at another pay phone. The manager of the phone company came down personally to help us out. He put a switchboard in the factory, with a total of twenty-six trunk lines, and people still couldn't get us. Haffa had to ask us to move out.'

Reynolds moved across the street, into what had once been an indoor tennis court owned by a vice-president of Marshall Field. It had been used during the war to make parts for Rolls-Royce aircraft engines. The Telephone Company ran fifty lines in there. Purchasing agents from all over the country crowded into the place, holding fleets of taxis outside to transport the merchandise they hoped to buy, and found that they were lucky to get even a handful of pens. One departmentstore manager, who flew in from San Francisco and pleaded unsuccessfully for pens, flew on to New York, stood in line at Gimbel's, bought two hundred pens at retail, and flew back with them to San Francisco, where he sold them at the price he had paid. Several would-be purchasers appealed to their senators to help them buy pens from Reynolds. The senators had to wait like the other supplicants to get a call through. 'My best friend, C. Gordon Anderson, who is president of the Richards Store Company, in Miami, wouldn't speak to me for two years after, because I didn't answer his wires,' Reynolds told me. 'I didn't even know he had sent any wires. Telegrams didn't mean a thing in that rush.' Mail sacks full of orders were piled up halfway to the ceiling in Printasign's offices. One day, a letter containing an order for a hundred and twenty-five thousand dollars' worth of pens tumbled out of one of the sacks. It had been postmarked three weeks earlier. Reynolds sat down in a near-by chair, stared at it thoughtfully, and concluded that one could be a happy victim of circumstances. Gimbel's, which had sold thirty thousand pens, including twelve thousand by mail, in the first week, was urging in its advertising of them, 'Write! Phone! Cable! Wire! Come!' By the end of his first month in the pen business, Reynolds, who at the outset had formally organized the Reynolds International Pen Company and capitalized it at twenty-six thousand dollars, had made a net profit, after taxes, of five hundred and forty-one thousand dollars.

By early 1946, Reynolds was turning out thirty thousand

pens a day and had eight hundred people working in his factory. (The personnel included three robust girls whose job it was to do nothing but inscribe with the same pen, in shifts, the words 'Write on the Ball, Reynolds Pen.' The idea was that they were to keep it up until the pen they were testing ran out of ink. The project was abandoned as unprofitable after three thousand foolscap pages had been covered with the slogan, and the girls were transferred to more creative work.) Orders were arriving daily for as many as a hundred thousand pens. Reynolds told his staff to accept orders only from those who would pay cash in advance. During one ten-day period, he deposited checks for more than a million and a half dollars in his bank, all in payment for pens yet to be made. By the beginning of December, he had a backlog of orders for a million pens, valued at twelve and a half million dollars at retail. 'It was then that we began selling paper,' he says. 'The printing press could turn out what the factory couldn't. We printed numbered gift certificates entitling the holder to a pen — strictly in the order of precedence on the waiting list.' A hundred thousand dollars' worth of certificates were bought the first day they were offered. By March, 1946, Reynolds had three million dollars in his bank.

Throughout the nation, stationery stores that had managed to get hold of some ball-point pens were becoming targets for burglars. A shipment of ten thousand Reynolds pens disappeared while in the custody of the Railway Express Agency. Two hundred complimentary pens, each marked 'I Swiped This from Milton Reynolds,' were swiped from his factory and turned up for sale in a Chicago store. In the tougher districts of several cities, some stores were more or less openly dealing in nothing but stolen ball-point pens. Reynolds installed guards in his plant and a fluoroscope at the entrance, but the underworld had already infiltrated. In all, pens worth seven hundred and fifty thousand dollars were smuggled out of the tennis court piecemeal, including some that one gang assembled in a near-by basement prior to disposing of them in the ball-point-pen black market. Reynolds had expected the demand for ball-point pens to decline after Christmas. Instead, it continued to grow. By February, 1946, Gimbel's ball-point-pen sales had amounted to a million and a half dollars, and Reynolds' profit, after taxes, was $1,558,607.81. His company statement was audited by Price, Waterhouse & Co., which reported the volume of sales as 'substantial.'

Almost simultaneously with the production of his first pens, Reynolds brought a million-dollar suit against Eversharp, alleging restraint of trade. His lawyer was Thurman Arnold, the trust buster. Reynolds charged that Eversharp had coerced dealers into canceling orders for his product. Eversharp denied everything. 'Reynolds just brought the suit for publicity, of course, and nothing ever came of it,' Straus remarked to me some time later. 'After he started it, he got together with Carl Byoir, the public-relations man, and Byoir spread the news where every pen dealer could see Reynolds' name. Smartest thing I ever saw. I hired the Byoir outfit myself, later. Naturally, we told our lawyers to bring a countersuit for a million dollars — I don't remember what for. Nothing ever came of that, either.'

For almost a year, only Gimbel's had local rights to the sale of the Reynolds pen. Macy's didn't have the pen and was made to feel it, as Gimbel's advertised triumphantly, 'It would be Gimbel's (young in heart but old in years, almost 104) that would burst in with this incredible Buck Rogers baby!' Privately, Gimbel's was no less stirred. 'The ball-point pen captured Mr. Fred Gimbel's fancy the moment he saw it,' an executive of the store told me. 'A man of amazing imagination and courage, by the way. He snuck the Hearst collection away from Macy's, you know. Well, Mr. Fred made the Reynolds pen his personal baby. There were no other real gift items around in the Christmas traffic of '45. Lots of mink coats at six

thousand and up, plus luxury tax, but where were the stores on hosiery? Where were they on white shirts and toys? Frankly, there was too much second-quality merchandise. The ball-point pen was a godsend. Mr. Fred insisted that all the salespeople write their sales checks with the pen. He hammered at it.'

The Reynolds firm, in the course of a report on its financial position and prospects, in April, 1946, called attention to 'the many advances which Reynolds has pioneered in the development of the ball-point pen.' It also noted that purchasers of the pen sometimes let its faults detract from their appreciation of its novel features. 'Frankly,' the report stated, 'one of the problems which arose was the occasional development of a small air bubble in the barrel of the pen which sometimes prevented the free flow of ink to the ball point.' Unhappily, this embolismic flaw was proving almost endemic to Reynolds pens. And there were other disorders. Sometimes, when the pen was not gently used, the ball bearing fell out of the point and the ink, called Satinflo, spurted all over, and sometimes the ball bearing became clogged with particles of pigment and wouldn't function at all. Many Reynolds-pen owners found that, even in an unclogged state, the pen would write satisfactorily only when held at an almost ninety-degree angle to the paper. 'Other noticeable defects,' a pen man recalled, 'were skipping and directionality, or faintness of lines in one particular direction, and then there was gooping, too, or the deposition of large droplets of ink. Besides, of course, just plain failure to write.'

Because the parts were often fitted together imperfectly, the pen not only gooped, it plainly leaked. Gimbel's salesclerks, who demonstrated the pen in trays of water on the counter, spent much of their time rinsing Satinflo from their hands in trays of a special cleaner conveniently placed under it. Consumers' Research pronounced the ink 'a very fugitive dye, so fugitive indeed that it would seem that the greatest usefulness of the pen might be for persons who have reasons for wishing their writings to fade out rather quickly.' Reynolds customers, on the other hand, encountered considerable difficulty trying to make the ink fade from their clothing. Many complained that when they carried the pen in an inside pocket, the ink remorselessly rode up in the barrel under the influence of body heat and formed a bubble at the top that burst, with a soft squelching sound, spraying suits, shirts, and underwear. Many owners who had been thus put upon began sending Reynolds their cleaners' bills, and in some instances the damaged clothing itself. Nine times out of ten, the cleaning was a waste of money, for Satinflo proved to be impervious to most cleaning fluids. While Reynolds had guaranteed his pen, he had not guaranteed the clothing of people who wrote with it. Nevertheless, as a good-will measure, he paid the cleaners' bills and, at his own expense, turned the ink-stained clothing over to an enterprising Chicago cleaner who made a specialty of removing spots of Satinflo with a fluid of his own devising. The treated clothing, neatly pressed, was returned to the aggrieved customers. Reynolds' bills from this cleaner for a time amounted to several hundred dollars a week.

Cleaners' bills and ink-stained clothes were not the only things disgruntled customers sent to Reynolds. Defective pens began coming back to him at a brisk rate. Reynolds says that during the first eight months of production he replaced 104,643 faulty pens, including a considerable number ungraciously returned to him by people to whom he had presented them as gifts. 'We sincerely tried to improve the pen,' he says. 'The sad fact is that by the time we got the bugs out of it, it was time to get out of the pen business.'

Other pen manufacturers were denouncing the upstart pen. 'Take a look at the Constitution of the United States. You can't get that variety of signatures with a ball,' a representative of Waterman sneered in an interview with the press, apparently unaware that his firm was presently to bring out a ball-point pen of its own. The press also reported that Parker, which has never brought out a ball-point pen, had called the Reynolds 'the only pen that will make eight carbons and no original.' Straus, who was still discarding one laboratory model of his

148

pen after another, said nothing. He was not feeling very happy about either the Reynolds pen or the fact that Macy's had got hold of some original Biro pens from a South American distributor and was advertising them as 'the same pen people have been talking about, asking for.' Since these pens were imported, Macy's was not prevented by the O.P.A. from asking what it wanted for them, which it did — nineteen-ninety-eight.

Meanwhile, a number of new, smaller companies were mushrooming up to manufacture their versions of the ball-point pen, some of which very closely resembled Biro's. 'Everybody started infringing on our patents,' Straus told me, 'because they were under the impression that Reynolds had infringed on them and that if he could get away with it, they could. Unfortunately, Reynolds hadn't.' Straus yearned to sue the offenders, but was dissuaded from doing so by the galling realization that if he succeeded in putting them out of business, he would be handing Reynolds something of a monopoly. Eventually, Straus partially solved the problem by granting several of the manufacturers he suspected of infringement licenses to make ball-point pens under the Eterpen patents. One such concern was on the West Coast. 'I went out to this small infringer to tell them I was going to sue,' Straus recalled. 'When I got there, I found they were turning out the best ball-point pen I had ever seen, so I made a deal under which they would manufacture the pen for Eversharp. It came out as one of our later models and sold in the millions.'

Late in April, 1946, Eversharp finally got around to putting its own version of the Biro pen, called Eversharp CA (for 'capillary attraction'), on the market. It had been a long, slow birth. As early as the previous May, the company had heralded the pen's arrival with a cocktail party for the press in the St.

Regis. At the event, Ann Sheridan autographed a fan's glove with one of the pens, to prove its versatility; a small boy pounded another through a block of wood with a hammer, to prove its sturdiness; Eversharp scientists sealed a third in a vacuum jar, to prove that it wouldn't leak at an altitude of fifteen thousand feet, and then tossed it into a container of dry ice to prove that it would withstand subfreezing temperatures; and a Powers model posed with an eight-foot replica of the Eversharp CA in her arms, to prove that a Powers model can do anything. Two hundred complimentary pens were handed out to the press along with the cocktails. Everything was very festive, but after the party things bogged down in a morass of renewed difficulties with design and manufacture.

The Eversharp people had planned to undercut Reynolds by selling their pen for ten dollars, but when they at last saw it coming off the assembly line, they decided that it looked more expensive than his and set its price at fifteen. Reynolds was ready for the new arrival. On the day it appeared on the counters, he brought out a new model of his own pen and threw a cocktail-and-luncheon party at the Waldorf to introduce it. It was called the 400 and, unlike both his original model and the Eversharp pen, had, instead of a cap, a retractable protector that slid over the ball point. Girls in ballet costumes posed with the new pens beneath a twelve-foot replica of it. The press received five hundred free 400's. It was announced that the pen (which cost Reynolds sixty cents to make) would retail, like his first model, at twelve dollars and fifty cents.

The Eversharp pen was available at Macy's and the Reynolds 400 at Gimbel's.

'The smoothest writing ball-point pen we've ever seen!' cried Macy's. 'Reloads with a cartridge in fifteen seconds!'

(The Reynolds pen had to be sent back to the factory for re-filling.)

'This pen is the most unusual writing instrument of civilized times,' shrieked Gimbel's. 'A pen without a cap. Sounds fantastic, doesn't it? . . . The new Reynolds is, is, is!'

Macy's guaranteed the Eversharp pen to write 'up to' three years without refilling. ('Depending on how much you write,' Macy's added, in small type.)

Gimbel's boldly guaranteed the Reynolds pen to write a flat four years.

Macy's silently rebuked Gimbel's by publicly pointing out that *its* salespeople were wearing white gloves while demonstrating Eversharps.

Both pens sold in overwhelming quantities. 'In New York City papers, the pen parade almost took the show away from Spring fashions,' *Editor & Publisher* reported. Faced by his first real competition, Reynolds decided to step up his public relations. He began sending free pens to prominent and/or photogenic people here and abroad. He sent President Truman two hundred, each inscribed 'I Swiped This from Harry S. Truman,' and he sent lesser quantities of pens to every senator, congressman, and Supreme Court justice, as well as to many bank and insurance-company presidents. He presented the entire French Assembly, and every ambassador and minister in Washington, with Reynolds pens. In a single day, he distributed twenty-five hundred pens at a New York convention of the National Retail Dry Goods Association. He established two philanthropic organizations — the Reynolds Hole-in-One Association, which in the course of the next two years gave free pens to four thousand hole-in-one and double-eagle golfers, and the Reynolds Master Bowlers Association, which gave a pen to any tournament bowler who scored two hundred and seventy-eight or over. He offered newspaper editors a free pen for every story their papers carried that mentioned Reynolds pens. Every prominent radio comedian got one, and the promise of another for every joke he broadcast about ball-point pens. Most of the resulting gags, which for a time threatened to choke the air waves, dealt with the underwater aspects of ball-point pens. They reached their climax in a skit in the revue *Make Mine Manhattan*, in which a comedian, pen in hand and clad in shorts and undershirt, was pushed into a tank of water by a salesman.

To open up foreign markets, Reynolds flew around the world in commercial airliners. Upon his return, he reported that while shaving over the Atlantic he had closed a deal for a hundred thousand pens with an eager jobber in the China-coast trade; that while changing shirts over the Pacific he had sold another hundred thousand to two Australian merchants; and that while riding into San Francisco in an airline bus he had taken an order for twenty-five thousand pens from the owner of forty Australian department stores. In all, he brought back orders for half a million pens. By the late summer of 1946, Reynolds pens were being sold in thirty-seven foreign countries, as well as on Pitcairn Island, where descendants of Captain Bligh's mutineers were busily weaving baskets — in lieu of money, of which they have little — to pay Reynolds for a consignment of pens they had ordered. In Hong Kong, the pens were selling for seventy-five dollars in American money and were widely used as a medium of exchange. An explorer back from the upper Amazon reported that he had successfully negotiated hostile Indian territory by handing out ball-point pens to the natives. The pens were blamed for a trade depression in Hiroshima, because of a slump in the sale of writing brushes, one of the principal products of the city.

Back home, Reynolds bought a plane, hired a pilot, and made a flying sales tour of the United States. Frequently, he would be greeted at a municipal airport by the managers of the local department stores, who rushed out onto the landing field waving orders. On a number of occasions when Reynolds was signing a sales contract, the ball-point pen he was using failed, creating a situation that lesser men might have found awkward. Reynolds never faltered. When a pen failed, he would contemptuously toss it aside and draw another from his pocket, like an arrow from a quiver. As at least one of the pens in his reserve supply was almost sure to be a gooper, if not a leaker, he also ran through a vast number of suits.

A new trouble developed. Banks complained that the pens were an invitation to forgers, as the signatures on checks written with them could be transferred to documents by the pressure of a thumb on the script. The Corn Exchange Trust Company of New York warned its branch managers against the pen. On top of this, it became public knowledge that Clarence W. Windhell, then an executive of the New Jersey Treasury Department's Division of Purchase and a man to whom Reynolds had sent a complimentary pen, had cautioned the employees in the five hundred state offices under his jurisdiction not to use ball-point pens, on the ground that the ink was subject to fading. 'At first, the complaints were wonderful publicity,' a Gimbel's man recalled. 'People began wondering what kind of pen it was that made the banks mad, and for a few days our sales improved. But not for long.'

Reynolds deployed to Miami to take counteraction. There, in the presence of the press and Ruth Byrd, the Miami Beach

153

Queen of Sun and Fun, he signed a check for a hundred thousand dollars in a tray of water and promised to make it out to some charity if, after the check reposed for a year in the vault of the Mercantile National Bank of Miami Beach, his signature should be found to have faded. (When the year was up, he retrieved his underwater check. His signature had not faded. Reynolds partisans were jubilant. 'People were inclined to overlook the fact that the signature on the check, being locked in a vault, where the light couldn't get at it, couldn't fade anyway,' a former associate of Reynolds gratefully observed.)

But the adverse criticism was hurting Reynolds, and in October, 1946, he brought out a new model, called the Rocket, guaranteed to write for fifteen years, or thirty-two miles, nonstop. The Rocket came in 'six gorgeous colors — stratosphere blue, atomic red, radar green, jet black, chute silver, and cosmic gold,' and sold for three-eighty-five. It cost about thirty cents to make. Reynolds sent one of the Rockets to a lifer at Sing Sing, and Gimbel's put them on sale in forty departments, including Furniture. 'It didn't go so well,' Reynolds said to me. 'Our profits dropped to about three hundred and fifty thousand dollars a month.'

Competition was steadily increasing, too. By the Christmas season of 1946, approximately a hundred manufacturers were turning out ball-point pens, some of them selling for as little as two-ninety-eight. At Gimbel's, customers were returning defective Reynolds pens which they had bought for twelve dollars and fifty cents and were receiving in exchange new Rockets and eight dollars and sixty-five cents in cash. Macy's responded by offering an allowance of three dollars on any ball-point pen for which the owner had paid at least three dollars and a half, to be deducted from the price of any ball-point pen in stock priced at twelve dollars and a half or more. 'Do you own a horse and buggy ball-point pen?' Macy's asked in an advertisement. Gimbel's retorted the next day, 'When Johnny-come-lately tries to put Johnny-on-the-spot, WHAT HAPPENS?' and went on to offer an allowance of four dollars, to be deducted from the price of a pen of the customer's choice, on any unsatisfactory fountain pen of any kind, purchased anywhere, provided its purchase price had been at least eight dollars. *Women's Wear Daily* published a report that 'both stores were hoping the controversy could be extended because of its attendant publicity value.' An armistice was reluctantly declared when Eversharp threatened to bring suit against both stores, claiming that the advertisements had damaged its trade reputation.

Shortly before Christmas of 1946, Reynolds put out a Rocket Threesome set, consisting of a Rocket and two new models, the Rockette and the Stubby Rocket. The set was priced at nine-ninety-five. It didn't sell well. One morning in the middle of February, 1947, Macy's startled the world by running a large advertisement offering, 'for the first time anywhere,' the Reynolds Rocket Threesome for two-seventy-nine, or the pens in it for ninety-eight cents apiece. Macy's, which had got the pens not from Reynolds but from a Chicago jobber who had got them from Reynolds, sold sixty thousand of them the first day. 'What a blast!' a Macy's man said later. 'It took Gimbel's a day to get back on their pins.' Twenty-four hours after the Macy coup, Gimbel's advertised the Rocket Threesome at two-fifty-nine, or ninety-four cents per pen. 'Or, if you prefer,' Good Old Gimbel's added ominously, 'we recommend the B 2 Ballero (made by Blythe), which we consider a far superior pen in the lower-priced pen field.' The price war was intensified during the day. 'We were shopping Macy's every twenty minutes,' a Gimbel's executive recalls. 'The prices changed five times during shopping hours.' Before the day was over, Gimbel's began to run out of Threesome pens, which it had finally reduced to eighty-four cents. Word of the Threesome shortage at Gimbel's was not long in reaching Macy's, which reacted swiftly. According to one Macy's man, a number of the store's employees were immediately detached from their regular duties, given quantities of folding money, and instructed to head over to Gimbel's and buy up all Threesomes in sight. As soon as Gimbel's was cleaned out of Threesomes at eighty-four cents, Macy's, which had knocked theirs down to eighty-eight cents, shot the price back to ninety-eight cents. The next day, Gimbel's rallied. It placed on sale three models — Junior, Senior, and Super Rockets — which Reynolds had just brought out to sell at a dollar sixty-nine each. Gimbel's charged only eighty-eight cents for them. Reynolds heard about this and sadly said he might be obliged to sue his old friend Gimbel's for cutting the price of models that had only just gone on the market. Gimbel's restored the new Rockets to the price Reynolds had set.

Relations between Reynolds and Gimbel's were never the same after that mention of B 2 Ballero. On February sixteenth, Gimbel's, proclaiming itself 'the granddaddy of the ball-point pen business,' publicly expressed the belief that 'there is no bigger ball-point pen value than the Rolls by Continental,' priced at ninety-eight cents.

It was time to get himself in the public eye again, Reynolds decided. Calling in the press, he passed out pens to all hands and announced that he would shortly fly around the world with William P. Odom, a veteran of flying the Hump into China. Reynolds said he was out to break the record time of ninety-one hours and fourteen minutes, set by Howard Hughes in 1938. He said that he would act as navigator of the plane, an A-26 light attack bomber, which he had bought and converted for the flight and had christened the Reynolds Bombshell. After several delays, in the course of which Reynolds reduced from a hundred and ninety-one pounds to a hundred and sixty-one, so that he could squeeze through the narrow cabin door, he took off from LaGuardia Field on April twelfth, seated facing backward in a makeshift jump seat, between the pilot and co-pilot, and gallantly flourishing a fistful of ball-point pens, all guaranteed not to leak at twenty thousand feet. Four days later, he was back at LaGuardia, having broken the Hughes record by twelve hours and nineteen minutes, and having given away a thousand pens en route. The trip cost two hundred and fifty-five thousand dollars, and Reynolds considered the publicity he received worth every penny of it. 'My press-clipping-service bill alone came to twenty thousand dollars,' he reported later. Reynolds and Odom made a triumphal appearance at the White House, where Mr. Truman congratulated them on their achievement. 'The President was very gracious,' Reynolds says. 'He said he had followed the flight all the way around on the radio. He told me a funny story about his grandmother and asked me how business was in general. I said I didn't know much about business in general but that I was doing all right.'

The heroes returned to New York, where Reynolds, to the surprise of the pen world, put in an appearance not at Gimbel's but at Macy's, which celebrated the occasion by announcing the exclusive sale of a brand-new two-pointed Reynolds model—'The only pen that writes in red and blue! Actually, two pens in one!' The hydra-headed pen, which was priced at ninety-eight cents, was, naturally, named the Bombshell, and Reynolds, using one, freely dispensed autographs to the awed customers. Gimbel's took it very hard. 'We had thought *we* were all set to break the Bombshell before Milton started off on the trip,' a Gimbel's man complained later. 'We even sent a box of K rations to him at the Gotham to take along with him. Then — think of it! — he brought the Bombshell out over *there*. And we'd already put a big ad in the *Times* congratulating him! Mr. Fred was very, very put out.'

The year 1947 was a lean one for ball-point-pen manufacturers. The public didn't respond properly to round-the-world flights, or to two pens in one, or to any of the numerous incantations with which Reynolds and the other manufacturers sought to stir it. Eversharp, which had finally paid more than a million dollars to buy out Eterpen's American rights in their entirety, lost over three million dollars that year. In an apologia to the firm's stockholders, Straus, who has since resigned its presidency, hinted that perhaps he and his colleagues had allowed themselves to become too deeply impressed by what had seemed an insatiable demand for ball-point pens. 'Your management,' he wrote, 'expended so great a portion of its time and attention in solving the problems of the ball-point pen that certain developments of its conventional . . . business were, perhaps, underemphasized.' One Eversharp official has since, in more succinct language, pointed out another difficulty that was besetting the trade then. 'The monkeys took over,' he said. 'Predatory individuals on the tail of a fast item. People were parking their cars in the street and using their garages as ball-point-pen factories. Their pens, of course, were inferior.'

Reynolds was having as many difficulties as the rest of them, but he refused to be downcast. His faith in airplane flights as a means of stimulating sales remained unflagging. In December of the year that Eversharp found so disappointing, he announced that he would lead a large expedition to China with the object of finding and measuring a mountain that was rumored to be higher than Mount Everest, in the Amne Machin Range, near the Chinese-Tibetan border. The expedition, he said, was to be undertaken with the co-operation of the Boston Museum of Science, the Army, the Air Force, Harvard, and the Academia Sinica, a Chinese-government scientific society, and would also explore the unmapped sources of the Yellow River. He had bought another plane, he continued — a C-87, which he had christened the Explorer — to fly the expedition over, and it was to be piloted by Odom. 'On board,' the *Times* reported, 'besides Mr. Reynolds, pen manufacturer and sportsman, [will be] geologists, meteorologists, photographers, and physicists, as well as radar equipment, special height-measuring apparatus, cameras, thermometers, and a battery of delicate and precise barometers.' The Chinese government agreed to let Reynolds make the flight, provided he took some Chinese scientists along with him. Interviewed in Nanking, Dr. Adam Pentung Sah, director general of the Academia Sinica, said the expedition would be welcome. He also remarked that Chinese geologists already had the sources of the Yellow River well in hand and had determined the highest peak in the Amne Machin Range to be no more than twenty thousand feet, approximately ten thousand feet less than Mount Everest. 'Actually, it was *Life* magazine that put me up to it,' Reynolds said later. 'They called me up and asked if I wanted to hunt for this highest mountain, which, by a coincidence, I had been reading up on. They said their science editor had been working on the problem for a whole year. I asked them why they didn't run their own expedition. They said they just printed the news, they didn't make it.'

The expedition took off from Oakland, California, early in March, 1948, in a gratifying swirl of publicity. Before leaving, Reynolds had an audience with President Truman, received his best wishes for success, and, in return, assured him that he would do his utmost 'to keep the United States in the lead of scientific research.' He also arranged to have the President supplied with more pens. Upon arriving in China, Reynolds became involved in a series of differences with the Chinese, who demanded that a considerable — and, it seemed to Reynolds, unreasonable — number of their scientists accompany him on the trip. Between wrangles, Reynolds held press conferences. In Shanghai, wearing the uniform of a war correspondent, he received the press in the Hotel Cathay and displayed credentials from *Life;* in Peiping, in the Grand Hotel des Wagons-Lits, he appeared in a blue mandarin costume and handed out pens to Chinese reporters, some of whom sold them on the black market as soon as the conference was over. The Shanghai *Evening Post & Mercury* impatiently suggested that the expedition hurry up with the job of finding the world's highest mountain, which it proposed, somewhat facetiously, be named Mount Reynolds. Reynolds, who was planning to issue a special Explorer pen if he found the mountain, was delighted with the proposal and sent the editor a ball-point perfume dispenser (a Reynolds side line) which was guaranteed to exude scent for five years. The perfume was one called Trois Fleurs, and Reynolds smelled overpoweringly of it, for he also carried a number of the dispensers in his pockets and they, like the pens, had a tendency to leak.

Finally, Reynolds got things more or less straightened out

with the Chinese, and the great day for the flight over the Amne Machin Range arrived. The Explorer, heavily loaded with American and Chinese scientists, its crew, and Reynolds, set off down a runway outside Peiping. Suddenly it tilted, its right propeller touched the ground, its nose wheel collapsed, and it gently settled into the mud of China. Nobody was hurt. 'The expedition is over,' Reynolds announced gravely as he surveyed the damage. 'Captain Everest has won again.'

Two days later, with a crew but without scientists, either American or Chinese, Reynolds and the Explorer landed at the Shanghai airport. He told Chinese reporters that his plane had been repaired at Peiping by mechanics of the Chinese Air Force and that he was leaving immediately for the United States, via Tokyo. Fourteen hours later he landed again, without explanation, at the Shanghai airport. When word of this reached Dr. Bradford Washburn, director of the Boston Museum of Science, who had accompanied Reynolds to China as a member of the expedition and was still in Shanghai, he exclaimed, 'Well, I'll curl up and die! He must have flown over the Amne Machin Range!' Reynolds denied this. 'We were on our way to India,' he said. 'Then we realized we didn't have the necessary visas and came back.'

In Nanking, Dr. Sah, who appeared to regard it as significant that the cruising speed of Reynolds' plane was two hundred miles an hour, or just about right to get from Shanghai to the Amne Machin Range and back in fourteen hours, charged Reynolds with a 'deliberate violation of his agreement with the Chinese government' and said he would file a protest with the American Embassy. Accompanied by eight similarly distressed Academia Sinica colleagues, Dr. Sah then called on Reynolds, who had proceeded to Nanking. 'We feel rather heavy hearted at what you have been doing since the accident at Peiping. We do not feel you have conducted yourself as the leader of a great expedition should,' Dr. Sah said. Reynolds, chain-smoking cigarettes in an amber holder, again denied having flown over the range but admitted 'negligence' in having taken off without informing the scientists. Observing that his callers seemed unimpressed by his denial, he offered to set up a ball-point-pen factory in China, all profits to go to the New Life Movement Association, an organization devoted to the betterment of China. He glowingly referred to the Chinese Air Force as 'one of the greatest little air forces in the world,' and said he would gladly lead a new expedition of Chinese scientists to the Amne Machins.

The interview broke up inconclusively and Reynolds returned to Shanghai. There he found his plane, with Odom and the rest of the crew inside it, impounded and guarded by Chinese armed with tommy guns. Reynolds' passport was taken away from him, and he was ordered to report to the local police station. He said later that he believed he was about to be shot. He took emergency action. Strolling over to the guards, he casually suggested that they let him enter the plane to get them some ball-point pens. Permission was granted. Reynolds climbed into the plane and hurled out handfuls of gold-plated pens. Then, while the guards were scrambling for them, he slammed the door and told Odom to gun the engines, and the plane roared off down the runway for Tokyo. Including those he tossed out of the plane, Reynolds had given away ten thousand pens in China.

'I'm through with China. Now we are back in God's country,' Reynolds told the press, between bites into a hot dog, upon his arrival at the Tokyo airport. After a pause, he added, 'At least, Americans run it.'

Reynolds flew back to the United States by easy stages, pursued by cries of 'Impostor!' from the Chinese press. Dr. Sah wrote a letter to the *New York Times*, in which he called the expedition a failure and deplored the wasting of the energies of several Chinese geologists 'at a time when they are carrying out such projects as the study of glaciation of the lower Yangtze.' *Time*, without mentioning the role its sister publication had played in the fiasco, reviewed the affair in curt and liverish fashion. A member of the Associated Press staff in Shanghai flew back and forth over the Amne Machin Range in a radar-equipped plane and reported, 'If there's a peak there higher than Everest we couldn't find it.' The Moscow radio implied that Reynolds had actually been hunting for uranium on behalf of American imperialism.

Reynolds has since told friends, and various Lions Club luncheon groups, which hold him in high regard as a speaker, that he and the plane's crew did fly over the Amne Machin Range. 'The mountain was there, all right,' he has said. 'It was covered with snow. A magnificent sight! We were flying at more than twenty-seven thousand feet and its peak disappeared into the clouds at thirty-one thousand feet.' On other occasions, in a less exuberant mood, he has said of his venture into the Orient, 'I lost face.' A close friend of Reynolds' told me that Reynolds once showed him some hazy motion pictures, taken in the air, of a tall mountain. 'Unfortunately, there was no way of telling from the movie how high the mountain was,' the friend added. 'You have to know Milt to appreciate the situation. He spent a lot of money to find a mountain higher than Everest, and I'm absolutely convinced he thinks he found one.'

The expedition cost Reynolds two hundred and fifty thousand dollars, and he had almost nothing except lost face to show for it. Back in Chicago, he found little to cheer him. His newest pen, the Reynolds Flyer, was selling for a measly thirty-nine cents retail. The pen now cost about eight cents to manufacture, allowing Reynolds a margin of profit that he considered negligible. Accordingly, he called his staff together, remarked briskly that they had no tradition to carry on, and, except for retaining a few relatively minor foreign holdings, quietly went out of the pen business. The Reynolds Hole-in-One Association and the Reynolds Master Bowlers' Association were similarly dissolved. Shortly thereafter, the Moscow radio announced that production of a ball-point pen would soon begin at the Sacco & Vanzetti Pencil Factory, in Moscow.

Reynolds emerged from the pen business a millionaire. He still hands out free pens, most of which he has made up for him by a former employee now in business for himself, at the rate of about thirty a week, to bellboys, hotel clerks, people he meets at parties, and traffic cops who stop him for speeding. Part of the year he lives in a four-room suite in a big hotel off Chicago's South Shore Drive, surrounded by Napoleonic chairs and prints and twenty-six books of selected press clippings, handsomely bound, and part of the year he spends at a country club near Mexico City, where, as a side line, he controls several land-holding companies. Reynolds picked up a seventeenth-century château near Versailles in 1947 but has seldom visited it. 'I bought the place when I was in the pen business. They told me it was a steal,' he said to me once, as he showed me photographs of the château. 'It has *two* moats — gee! — gardens, statues and everything! It couldn't be replaced for millions. I turned the stables into a ball-point-pen assembly plant.'

Reynolds still likes to travel. Late in 1949, he tried to beat the record for a round-the-world flight on scheduled airlines, a record then held by Colonel Edward Eagan, former chairman of the New York State Athletic Commission. Flying eastward from Los Angeles, Reynolds crossed Europe and passed through Damascus, Karachi, Delhi, Calcutta, Bangkok, Hong Kong, Manila, Guam, and Midway on schedule, but he missed a connection at Honolulu and gave up the attempt, saying dispiritedly, 'I'll never try again.'

But one day three years later, when he turned up, tanned, highly vocal, and richer than ever, at the Gotham Hotel in New York, I could see right away, from the new international airlines labels on his luggage, that he had been at it again. He was wearing a conservative blue suit, a checkered vest, a blue and yellow tie bearing his initials in baroque script, and a pair of gold cuff links engraved with a Hindu motto which he said meant 'I Fight For Bundi.' He told me that, by way of extending a trip with his wife to India to hunt tigers with the Maharajah of Bundi, who'd given him the cuff links, he'd completed his sixth round-the-world flight. He and the Maharajah had initially met on a plane somewhere between New Delhi and Calcutta in 1946, when Reynolds was selling pens on his first round-the-world flight. Reynolds gave the Maharajah a ballpoint pen that worked, they became chummy, and repeated invitations to the Maharajah's palace in Bundi followed until Reynolds finally gave in. The former ball-point-pen king was impressed with the standard of living at the Maharajah's palace. 'Straight out of King Solomon! What a setup! Three hundred household servants! We ate wild boars for breakfast!' he said. Then he went on to describe how, at the Maharajah's tiger hunt, he, Reynolds, had repeatedly blazed away at and finally bagged a tiger, possibly a man-eater, the head of which the Maharajah was now having stuffed for mounting on the wall of

165

Reynolds' apartment in Chicago. Reynolds went on to remark that he hoped the Maharajah's taxidermist had remembered to impart to the tiger's mouth a vicious snarl. Turning the conversation from tigers to money, I asked Reynolds how business was. He told me that he was making a nice thing of an electrical-equipment company, of which he was the largest stockholder. In 1946, he took a hundred and twenty-five thousand dollars — a small fraction of his ball-point-pen profits — and invested it in a hundred and twenty five thousand shares of the electrical company. He said that he was now getting a hundred and fifty thousand dollars a year in dividends from the investment, and that the stock was worth a million and a half. 'I'm doing all right,' Reynolds said. He absent-mindedly rummaged around in a suitcase and handed me genuine Reynolds ball-point pens — one that wrote in purple, one that wrote in blue and red, one that wrote in green, blue, red, and purple, one that glowed in the dark, and one, rather dusty, inscribed, 'I Swiped This from Major General Harry J. Vaughan.'

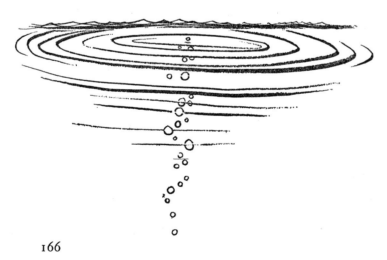